高等职业教育智能交通技术运用专业规划教材

交通运输职业教育教学指导委员会
交通运输管理类专业指导委员会　组织编写

English for Intelligent Transportation Systems
智能交通专业英语

梁伯栋　主　编
程　俊　副主编
齐　力[公安部第三研究所]　主　审

人民交通出版社股份有限公司
China Communications Press Co.,Ltd.

内 容 提 要

本书按照智能交通系统及其先进的交通管理系统、先进的出行者信息系统、先进的车辆控制系统、先进的公共运输系统,以及商用车辆运营系统5个子系统将内容分为6大单元。编写时在参考原版英文教材、期刊、论文、法律法规、产品说明,甚至新闻报道的基础上,积极吸取国内外其他专业英语教材的优点和基础英语课教学的经验,每个单元中均配有3篇英文课文和阅读材料,以着重介绍智能交通各研究领域的基本概念、原理、方法和应用。为了便于学习,每个单元中每篇课文和阅读材料后均列出文中出现的生词短语和配套练习。在本书末尾还附有交通运输专业常用的词汇术语和英语基础语法,以供学生参考。

本书既可作为智能交通类相关专业的"专业英语"课程教材、"智能交通系统"课程的双语教材,以及有关专业继续教育及职业培训教材,也可作为智能交通行业的管理人员和科技工作者自学及科研的参考用书。

图书在版编目(CIP)数据

智能交通专业英语 / 梁伯栋主编. —北京:人民交通出版社股份有限公司,2015.2
高等职业教育智能交通技术运用专业规划教材
ISBN 978-7-114-11752-7

Ⅰ.①智⋯ Ⅱ.①梁⋯ Ⅲ.①交通运输管理—智能系统—英语—高等职业教育—教材 Ⅳ.①H31

中国版本图书馆 CIP 数据核字(2014)第 227186 号

高等职业教育智能交通技术运用专业规划教材

书　　名:	智能交通专业英语
著 作 者:	梁伯栋
责任编辑:	司昌静　任雪莲
出版发行:	人民交通出版社股份有限公司
地　　址:	(100011)北京市朝阳区安定门外外馆斜街3号
网　　址:	http://www.ccpress.com.cn
销售电话:	(010)59757973
总 经 销:	人民交通出版社股份有限公司发行部
经　　销:	各地新华书店
印　　刷:	北京鑫正大印刷有限公司
开　　本:	787×1092　1/16
印　　张:	10
字　　数:	230 千
版　　次:	2015年2月　第1版
印　　次:	2021年9月　第3次印刷
书　　号:	ISBN 978-7-114-11752-7
定　　价:	28.00 元

(有印刷、装订质量问题的图书由本公司负责调换)

智能交通技术运用专业规划教材编委会

编委会主任：鲍贤俊

编委会副主任：楼伯良　向怀坤

委　　　员：（按姓氏笔画排序）

刘国峰　纪玉国　严石林　严　玮

吴兆明　张春雨　李长霞　李吟龙

李　锐　陈　斌　周庚信　施建年

曹成涛　阎子刚　黄君麟　谭任绩

前　言

近年来，智能交通行业及其产业在我国得到了前所未有的快速发展，在保障交通安全、提高运输效率、缓解交通拥堵、降低环境污染、提升公众出行服务等各个方面发挥着日益重要的作用。特别是进入互联网时代以来，智能交通已经成为物联网、智慧城市建设的首要着陆点和代表性行业，迎来了蓬勃发展的历史机遇。

随着智能交通作为一个独立的产业迅速崛起，各级政府和企业都把发展智能交通作为提高竞争能力和提高企业核心竞争力的重要手段，在国家《道路交通安全"十二五"规划》、《道路交通科技发展"十二五"规划》以及《交通运输行业智能交通发展战略(2012—2020年)》等多部文件中，对我国智能交通行业及产业的发展给予了明确的支持。

行业要发展首要是人才，智能交通正强烈呼唤着大批优秀人才破茧而出，向更新更高的技术和管理领域集聚。为实现人才培养目标，适应我国智能交通行业的发展需求，培养面向生产、建设、服务和管理第一线需要的智能交通行业的高技能人才，推动高职课程建设与改革，加强教材建设，交通运输管理类专业指导委员会在全国交通运输职业教育教学指导委员会的指导下，根据2013年教育部颁布的《交通安全与智能控制专业教学标准与课程标准》(适应于高等职业教育)，精心组织全国从事高职教学第一线的优秀教师和企业专家，合作编写了交通安全与智能控制专业系列教材，供高职高专院校交通安全与智能控制专业教学使用。

本书的编写特点：

1.在资料来源上，本书参考大量与智能交通相关的原版英文教材、期刊、论文、报告，甚至网页。内容新颖、选题广泛且可读性强，对提高读者的智能交通类英文阅读能力有很大帮助。

2.在编写内容上，为强化各章内在的连贯性和系统性，按照智能交通系统及其子系统划分和安排各章内容。在各章均配以3篇英文阅读材料，着重介绍智能交通各研究领域的基本概念、原理、方法和应用。为了便于学习，各章每篇阅读材料后均列出生词短语和配套练习。在本书末尾还附有交通运输专业常用的词汇术语和英语基础语法，以供读者参考。

3.在编写团队上，体现"校企合作"与"专兼结合"。本书主编为高职教育教学一线专任教师，副主编为行业企业一线技术骨干，参编为同类各高职院校教育教学一线专任教师。这种教材编写团队可以充分利用学校与企业的优势,有利于编写更适合工作岗位职业能力需求的教学用书。

参加本书编写工作的有:深圳职业技术学院梁伯栋(编写 Chapter 1、Appendix 1、Appendix 2)、上海交通职业技术学院谢逸卿(编写 Chapter 2)、深圳职业技术学院毛海霞(编写 Chapter 3)、深圳职业技术学院胡松华(编写 Chapter 4)、北京交通运输职业学院高原(编写 Chapter 5、Appendix 3)、中国科学院深圳先进技术研究院程俊(编写 Chapter 6)。深圳职业技术学院学生何景奎、何结红、徐涛、练玲、曾丽婷参与了 Chapter 1 中和 Chapter 6 中的 New Words and Expressions 部分的编写,在此一并致谢。

全书由梁伯栋担任主编并负责统稿,程俊担任副主编,公安部第三研究所齐力担任主审。

本套教材在编写过程中参阅和引用了国内外相关的论著和资料,无论在参考文献中是否列出,在此,对这些文献的作者和译者表示由衷的感谢和诚挚的谢意。

由于作者水平有限,书中不妥之处在所难免,恳请专家和读者给予批评和指正。

编者
2014 年 12 月

目 录

Chapter 1　Intelligent Transportation Systems(ITS) ……………………………………… 1
　1.1　The Evolution of Transport ……………………………………………………… 1
　　　　New Words and Expressions …………………………………………………… 6
　　　　Exercises ………………………………………………………………………… 7
　1.2　Introduction to ITS ……………………………………………………………… 8
　　　　New Words and Expressions ………………………………………………… 12
　　　　Exercises ……………………………………………………………………… 13
　1.3　Call for Papers IEEE-ITSC2013 ……………………………………………… 14
　　　　New Words and Expressions ………………………………………………… 17
　　　　Exercises ……………………………………………………………………… 17

Chapter 2　Advanced Transportation Management Systems(ATMS) ………………… 19
　2.1　Sensing Traffic Using Sensors ………………………………………………… 19
　　　　New Words and Expressions ………………………………………………… 27
　　　　Exercises ……………………………………………………………………… 28
　2.2　Traffic Surveillance and Management ………………………………………… 29
　　　　New Words and Expressions ………………………………………………… 32
　　　　Exercises ……………………………………………………………………… 33
　2.3　Electronic Toll Collection ……………………………………………………… 34
　　　　New Words and Expressions ………………………………………………… 40
　　　　Exercises ……………………………………………………………………… 41

Chapter 3　Advanced Traveler Information Systems(ATIS) …………………………… 43
　3.1　Overview of ATIS ……………………………………………………………… 43
　　　　New Words and Expressions ………………………………………………… 46
　　　　Exercises ……………………………………………………………………… 47
　3.2　Route Choice with Real-time Information …………………………………… 47
　　　　New Words and Expressions ………………………………………………… 50
　　　　Exercises ……………………………………………………………………… 51
　3.3　GIS and GPS in ITS …………………………………………………………… 52
　　　　New Words and Expressions ………………………………………………… 54
　　　　Exercises ……………………………………………………………………… 55

Chapter 4　Advanced Vehicle Control Systems(AVCS) ………………………………… 57
　4.1　Intelligent Vehicle Technology ………………………………………………… 57
　　　　New Words and Expressions ………………………………………………… 66
　　　　Exercises ……………………………………………………………………… 67
　4.2　The Self-Driving Car …………………………………………………………… 68
　　　　New Words and Expressions ………………………………………………… 73

    Exercises ·· 74
 4.3 Automatic Parking System ··· 75
    New Words and Expressions ·· 79
    Exercises ·· 79

Chapter 5 Advanced Public Transportation Systems(APTS) ···································· 81
 5.1 Urban Transit Definitions ··· 81
    New Words and Expressions ·· 84
    Exercises ·· 85
 5.2 Public Transportation Priority ·· 86
    New Words and Expressions ·· 88
    Exercises ·· 89
 5.3 Automatic Vehicle Location ·· 90
    New Words and Expressions ·· 92
    Exercises ·· 93

Chapter 6 Commercial Vehicle Operation Systems(CVOS) ······································· 95
 6.1 Intelligence in Transport Logistics ·· 95
    New Words and Expressions ·· 101
    Exercises ·· 101
 6.2 Challenges of CVOS ··· 102
    New Words and Expressions ·· 107
    Exercises ·· 108
 6.3 Electronic Screening System for the State of Missouri ·································· 108
    New Words and Expressions ·· 117
    Exercises ·· 118

Key to Exercises ·· 120
Appendix ··· 131
 1 Acronym ·· 131
 2 Glossary ·· 137
 3 Grammar ··· 141
References ··· 148

Chapter 1 Intelligent Transportation Systems (ITS)

1.1 The Evolution of Transport

Adapted from "The Evolution of Transport" by Jesse H. Ausubel and Cesare Marchetti, published in The Industrial Physicist, 7(2):20-24, April 2001.

Travel benefits from orientation-fixed points by which to navigate. Our aim is to provide some fixed points derived from a technical analysis of transport systems that enables us to understand past travel and prepare for its future. Along the way, the lunacy of popular ideas such as car pooling, telecommuting, and the revival of traditional railroads will become clear. Instead, we will offer something far more beautiful: a transport system emitting zero pollutants and sparing the surface landscape, while people on average range hundreds of kilometers daily on a system of "green" mobility.

In a spatially inhomogeneous system, living things are much favored by mobility. A couple of billion years ago bacteria were already equipped with rotating flagella, stirred by electric micromotors of the kind physicists call step motors, and even capable of traveling in reverse.

When a sufficient level of oxygen permitted multicellular architecture, mobility was assured with specialized structures, the muscles. Coordination of the distant muscles of an animal requires a central processing unit and fast wires to carry sensory inputs as well as operational orders. Predators develop in every ecosystem, including that of the monocellular organisms. The evolution of the nervous system, thus, responds to the need for management at a distance. The gazelle must be faster than the lion and have the chance to run. Human primacy in the biosphere is tied to the nervous system, and our development shows how much we owe to the necessity of mobility.

1.1.1 Four Instincts of Human Mobility

Human mobility stems from four basic instincts. These instincts permit analysts to create a simple model for the complex use that humans make of transport.

The first travel instinct is to stick to the budget of time dedicated to mobility. Humans reside in a protected base, be it a cave, a castle, or a high-rise apartment. Like all animals who have a protected base, we carefully measure the time in which we expose ourselves to the dangers of the external world, be they bears or drunken drivers. The late Yacov Zahavi measured travel time in the 1970s. The results were invariant, about one hour per day, measured over the year and the entire adult population. Recent measures give the same result from Australia to Zambia. California is higher than the U.S. average because Californians spend more time doing other things in their cars, including eating. Interestingly, the travel time budget was also about one hour 5,000 years ago. Telecommuting fails to save energy or reduce traffic because when we travel fewer minutes to work, we travel equally more minutes to shop or pursue leisure activities.

The second instinct is to return to the lair in the evening. When people depart from the home, the center of the human world, they use the best means of transport. The homing instinct lies at the core of the success of airlines. Airbus Industries found that about 60% of air passengers in Europe do their business and return on the same day, notwithstanding the higher fare. Shuttles operating from New York and Los Angeles carry a similar proportion of day-trippers. Revived and sustained at great cost, the trains between Boston, New York, and Washington still fail to accommodate a round trip within one day for most travelers. Thus the airlines, barely challenged, extract a high fare between New York and either of the other two cities.

The third instinct is to spend within the travel-money budget. Families everywhere spend about 12% ~ 15% of their disposable income for mobility. Zahavi measured the phenomenon 30 years ago, and data recently gathered show the same narrow range.

The fourth instinct originates in the fact that humans are territorial animals. The objective of territorial animals is to have as large a territory as possible within the natural limits of the possibilities to acquire and manage it. Most of human history is a bloody testimony to the instinct to maximize range.

For humans, a large accessible territory means greater liberty in choosing the three points of gravity of our lives: the home, the workplace, and the school. Four-fifths of all travel ends in this ambit.

1.1.2 Interpreting Movement

With this framework, we can begin to interpret the world of movement and the geography that forms its substrate. A person traveling by foot covers about 5 km in an hour. With a 1-hour travel budget to go and return home, a pedestrian's territory would have a radius of 2.5 km and, thus, an area of about 20 km^2. We can define this area as the territorial cell of the individual on foot. Topographic maps until about 1800 (and for much of the world today) showed territory that is tiled with cells of about 20 km^2, often with a village at the center.

When a village flourishes and becomes a city, the 20 km^2 territorial cell fills with people. However, its borders are not breached. Numerous examples of belts or walls of ancient cities show that they never exceeded 5 km in diameter. Even imperial Rome was 20 km^2. Vienna started with a small medieval wall, its Ring. Around 1700, after its victory against the Turks, Vienna built a second belt, the Guertel, which had a diameter of 5 km. Pedestrian Venice is elliptical, with a maximum diameter of about 5 km. Ancient Beijing measured 5 km × 10 km and thus seems to break the rule. However, close observation shows that Beijing was a double star—two adjacent cities, one Chinese and the other Mongol, separated by a wall with gates.

The travel situation remained the same until about 1800. There were horses, but few in proportion to potential riders. Horses reflected personal wealth, elevated militaries, and plowed fields. They did little for human mobility. Around 1815, Sweden topped the world in horse ownership with about 1 per 6 people, while Great Britain had about 1 per 10 and Belgium about 1 per 16. Most horses worked on farms. In the United States, where hay was inexpensive, the number of horses per capita peaked around 1900 at about 1 horse per 4 people. Compare that with the ratio today of 4 motor vehicles per 5 people.

Diocletian's Rome had about 1 million inhabitants at the beginning of the 4th century. Constantinople, Europe's largest city in 1700, had about 700,000. London, which would become first in population, had only 676,000 in 1750. In 1800, the great networks of roads created by the Romans still served much of Europe for the administrative messengers and the movement of troops and goods. Infantry made up the armies; cavalry were precious and rare.

1.1.3 Mobile Machines

Around 1800, new machines for transport entered the field and permitted ever-higher speeds, which revolutionized territorial organization. The highly successful machines are few—train, motor vehicle, and plane—and their diffusion slow. Each has taken from 50 to 100 years to saturate its niche. Each machine carries a progressive evolution of the distance traveled daily that significantly surpasses the 5 km of mobility by foot. Collectively, their outcome is a steady increase in mobility. For example, in the United States, from 1800 to today, mobility has grown an average of 2.7% per year, doubling every 25 years.

Since about 1920, when General Motors Corp. was formed, the auto has had an average speed in most countries of 35 to 40 km/h, derived by dividing all the kilometers that cars travel by all the hours they travel. Given that 1 h is the daily invariant of the traveler, and that car owners now use their autos for an average of 55 min a day, daily mobility in Europe, for example, is little more than 35 km/day.

The automobile and its mechanical cousins destroyed the village and invented the megalopolis. If the auto gives a mobility of about 35 km/h, then it affords a territory of about 1,000 km^2, 50 times the 20 km^2 of the pedestrian city. Mexico City, based on automobility, officially houses about 30 million people. One can interpolate Mexico City's development to a saturation of about 50 million around 2025. Fifty times the territory equals 50 times the population.

Today, in the developed countries, a motor vehicle stands by for nearly every licensed driver. The mode of transport is saturated. Carmakers can sell more cars, so we each have a second car at our second home or as fashion objects. However, adding cars will not increase our mobility because we have already hit the limit of our travel-time budget. Subways can flourish if they beat the average speed of the car, the 35 km/h door-to-door inclusive travel time. Surface mass transit such as buses, car pooling, and other modes that slow our inclusive travel time get rejected.

Environmentally, the one-license, one-car equation demands that autos on average must be clean. Incremental gains in the efficiency of internal combustion engines will not suffice. The alternative of a world fleet of 1 billion vehicles powered by huge batteries made with poisonous metals such as lead or cadmium poses materials recycling and disposal problems.

The obvious answer is the zero-pollutant fuel cell, in which compressed hydrogen gas mixes with oxygen from the air to give off electric current in a low-temperature chemical reaction that also makes water. When refiners direct their skills to making hydrogen, its cost should resemble that of gasoline. Moreover, the electrochemical process of the fuel cell is potentially 20% ~ 30% more efficient than the thermodynamic process of today's internal combustion engines. Ford and other manufacturers plan to produce 100,000 fuel-cell-powered autos annually within 10 years. Fuel-cell cars will take two to three decades to dominate the fleet because of the large investments in plants required, the 10-year average lifetime of cars, and gradual public acceptance. City air, now fouled mostly by cars, could be pristine by 2050.

1.1.4 Air Time

Cars will become cleaner but not faster. The state of technology permits a serious rise in mobility—that is, our average speed—only by augmenting time spent in the air. For all the hoopla about railroads, intercity trains move slowly. A good system, such as Germany's railroad, averages about 65 km/h and peaks at about 95 km/h measured as the distance between terminal points (as the falcon flies). The supreme trains, such as the French TGV, average about 150 km/h. Including the time to reach the station and board, trains are about as speedy as cars but lack the infinite frequency that car owners enjoy.

The mean speed of an airplane is 600 km/h, more than an order of magnitude faster than an auto, and planes are rapidly approaching cars in intercity passenger-kilometers transported. Still, in the United States, daily air time per person is only about 70 s, and Europeans average a scant 20 s daily.

Given that the authors travel on average about 30 min per day on airplanes, huge average increases can clearly occur without harming human health. However, the already inadequate air infrastructures would be violently stressed by a 25-fold rise in traffic in the United States or a 90-fold rise in Europe.

Until recently, the system evolved well by increasing, in proportion to the traffic, the productivity of planes— that is, the number of passenger-kilometers of flight, or the capacity per velocity. By replacing old planes with larger and faster ones, the commercial fleet long remained constant at around 4,000 planes, while passenger- kilometers increased 50-fold. In the past 15 years, however, the builders of airframes have feared to market super jumbo jets, which would cost perhaps \$ 10 billion for the first plane, because of the capital investment. Thus, the airlines make do with smaller craft, and the system has grown abruptly to about 9,000 planes and become horribly congested.

For the currently configured airports, the inevitable growth of high-speed transport will be hard. Looking out to 2050, our objective would be an airport that, without choking, handles 1 million passengers per day—8 to 10 times that of Los Angeles International Airport today. A drastic rethinking of passenger logistics can shrink the mess. Still, even with more efficient airports, environmental and safety problems loom.

In our outlook, airplanes will consume most of the fuel of the future transport system, a fact of interest to both fuel providers and environmentalists. Kerosene, today's jet fuel, will not pass current environmental tests at future air-traffic volumes. More hydrogen needs to enter the fuel mix, and it will, consistent with the gradual decarbonization of the energy system. Still, the transport system clearly needs a high-density mode having the performance characteristic of top airplanes without the problems.

1.1.5 New Travel Mode

The key is a new kind of transport. In the past 200 years, the system has embraced a new means of transport every 50 years or so: barges, trains, autos, planes. One can view these vehicles and their infrastructures as products competing for market share. The secular evolution is beautiful. Clearly, air will be the big winner for several decades. But the beginning of the millennium must also give birth to a new mode of transport. According to our studies, all bets are on magnetically levitated systems, or maglevs, a "train" with magnetic suspension and propulsion.

The maglev is a vehicle without a motor—thus, without combustibles aboard—and without wings and wheels, which is suspended magnetically between two guardrails that resemble an open stator of an electric motor. It is propelled by a magnetic field that, let's say, runs in front and drags it. The maglev is the perfect analog of a bunch of particles in an accelerator.

Hard limits to the possible speed of maglevs do not exist if the maglev runs in an evacuated tunnel, as the Swiss propose for Swissmetro, their future maglev railway system. "Evacuated" means simulating the low pressure that an airplane encounters at 10,000 to 20,000 m of altitude. Tunnels solve the problem of landscape disturbance and can also offer the straight lines that speed needs.

The maglev could break the weight rule—the rule of the ton—that has burdened mobility. The weight of a horse and its gear, a train, an auto, and a jumbo jet at takeoff are all about 1 ton of vehicle per passenger. The maglev could slim the weight to 300 kg, significantly dropping the energy cost of transport.

If room-temperature superconductors succeed, a braking vehicle could also almost totally recover its kinetic energy. The energy consumption of the trains would then basically result from pushing air out of the way. The aerodynamic losses of maglevs running in evacuated tubes, as in the Swiss plan, would decrease with lower air pressure and make the energy efficiency of high-speed transport zoom.

Maglevs offer the best way for electricity to further penetrate transport, the sector from which it has been largely excluded. French railroads, of course, are already powered cleanly and cheaply by nuclear electricity.

1.1.6 Mobility Picture

Finally, let us review our picture of mobility. Speed matters. Humans search for speed because, travel time being fixed, speed gives us territory, that is, access to resources. A person on foot has 20 km^2, a person in a car has 1,000 km^2, and the jet set has a continent. As a rule, the choice is to consume both the travel-budget hour and the disposable money budget, maximizing the distance, that is, the speed.

  The 21st century will come to be dominated by the maglev—from the office to the moon, to offer a motto. Consistent with basic instincts, maglevs can serve as the pinnacle of a super system for green mobility: cars powered by fuel cells, airplanes powered by hydrogen, and maglevs powered by electricity. Even the bacteria should be impressed with the mobility humans can achieve.

New Words and Expressions

lunacy [ˈluːnəsɪ]	n. 精神失常,愚蠢的行为
car pooling	拼车
revival [rɪˈvaɪv(ə)l]	n. 复兴,复苏
spatially [ˈspeɪʃ(ə)lɪ]	adv. 空间地
inhomogeneous [ˌɪnˌhəʊməˈdʒiːnɪəs]	adj. 不均匀的,不同类的
micromotor [maɪkrəˈməʊtər]	n. 微型电机
ecosystem [ˈiːkəʊˌsɪstəm]	n. 生态系统
monocellular [ˌmɒnoʊˈseljələr]	adj. 单细胞的
gazelle [ɡəˈzel]	n. 羚羊,瞪羚
biosphere [ˈbaɪəʊsfɪə(r)]	n. 生物圈
instinct [ˈɪnstɪŋkt]	n. 本能,天性
	adj. 充满着的
proportion [prəˈpɔː(r)ʃ(ə)n]	n. 比例
sustained [səˈsteɪnd]	adj. 持续的
testimony [ˈtestɪmənɪ]	n. 证词
pedestrian [pəˈdestrɪən]	n. 行人
radius [ˈreɪdɪəs]	n. 半径
topographic [ˌtɒpəˈɡræfɪk]	adj. 地形测量的
tiled [taɪld]	adj. 平铺的
medieval [ˌmedɪˈiːv(ə)l]	adj. 中世纪的
plow [plaʊ]	v. 犁地,耕地,开路
hay [heɪ]	n. 干草
capita [ˈkeɪpətə]	n. 头数(指牲口)
Diocletian	戴克里先(284-305年为罗马皇帝)
inhabitant [ɪnˈhæbɪtənt]	n. 居民
diffusion [dɪˈfjuːʒ(ə)n]	n. 扩散
saturate [ˈsætʃəreɪt]	adj. 浸透的,饱和的
	v. 浸透
flourish [ˈflʌrɪʃ]	v. 繁荣,兴旺
incremental [ˌɪnkrɪˈment(ə)l]	adj. 增值的
suffice [səˈfaɪs]	v. 足够,使满足
cadmium [ˈkædmɪəm]	n. 镉

current ['kʌrənt]	n. (电、水、气)流
	adj. 当前的,现在的
thermodynamic [ˌθɜː(r)məʊdaɪ'næmɪk]	adj. 热力学的
pristine ['prɪstiː]	adj. 原始的,新鲜的
augment [ɔːg'ment]	v. 增加
hoopla ['huːplɑː]	n. 喧嚣
terminal ['tɜː(r)mɪn(ə)l]	n. 终端,终端机;终点站,航站楼
	adj. 终点的
falcon ['fɔːlkən]	n. 猎鹰
supreme [sʊ'priːm]	n. 至高
	adj. 至高的
infinite ['ɪnfɪnət]	n. 无限,无穷
magnitude ['mægnɪtjuːd]	n. 大小,量级
infrastructure ['ɪnfrəˌstrʌktʃə(r)]	n. 基础设施;公共建设;下部构造
jumbo ['dʒʌmbəʊ]	n. 庞然大物
	adj. 巨大的
inevitable [ɪn'evɪtəb(ə)l]	adv. 必然地
choking ['tʃəʊkɪŋ]	adj. 令人窒息的
drastic ['dræstɪk]	adj. 猛烈的
logistics [lə'dʒɪstɪks]	n. 后勤
kerosene ['kerəsiːn]	n. 煤油
secular ['sekjʊlə(r)]	adj. 世俗的,长期的
millennium [mɪ'leniəm]	n. 千禧年
levitate ['levɪteɪt]	v. 使浮在空中
maglev ['mæglev]	n. 磁悬浮列车
propulsion [prə'pʌlʃ(ə)n]	n. 推进
combustible [kəm'bʌstəb(ə)l]	n. 可燃物
guardrail ['gɑːdreɪl]	n. 护栏,护轨
evacuate [ɪ'vækjueɪt]	v. 疏散,撤退
superconductor [ˌsupə(r)kən'dʌktə(r)]	n. 超导体
kinetic [kaɪ'netɪk]	adj. 运动的

Exercises

I. True or false

a) Human mobility stems from four basic instincts: to stick to the budget of time dedicated to mobility, to return to the lair in the evening, to spend within the travel-money budget, and to have as large a territory as possible.

b) The travel situation by foot remained the same until new machines for transport entered the field and permitted ever-higher speeds about 1800.

c) In Europe, daily air time per person is only about 20 s.

d) The fastest speed of the French TGV is 150 km/h.

e) According to author, new kind of future transport is maglev, a "train" with magnetic suspension and propulsion.

II. Choosing the best answer

a) What might be the dangers of the outside world? (   )

   A. budget   B. fare   C. bear   D. airbus

b) What is the meaning of "inhabitants"? (   )

   A. horses   B. coins   C. km^2 D. population

c) What should be considered in development of fuel-cell cars? (   )

   A. plants   B. lifetime of cars

   C. public acceptance   D. All

d) What is power by airplane? (   )

   A. gas   B. kerosene   C. diesel   D. fuel cell

e) What is a new mode of transport in 2000? (   )

   A. train   B. airplane   C. bus   D. maglev

III. Translation

a) Our aim is to provide some fixed points derived from a technical analysis of transport systems that enables us to understand past travel and prepare for its future.

b) In 1800, the great networks of roads created by the Romans still served much of Europe for the administrative messengers and the movement of troops and goods.

c) The alternative of a world fleet of 1 billion vehicles powered by huge batteries made with poisonous metals such as lead or cadmium poses materials recycling and disposal problems.

1.2 Introduction to ITS

In contemporary society, automobiles play an indispensable role in transporting people and goods. However, our transportation system is facing significant challenges, from traffic-related fatalities and injuries, congested roadways and rising gas prices to deteriorating infrastructure, increasing costs and shrinking financial budgets. With a growing population challenging an already strained transportation system, we cannot simply continue to increase the capacity of the current transportation system enough to meet demand.

To deal with them, across the world research and development is underway into systems that link road infrastructure and telecommunications using computers, electronics, and advanced sensing technologies.

ITS, standing for either intelligent transportation systems or intelligent transport systems, offer the concept and approach. ITS technologies enable us to make better use of the transportation network we already have while building smarter infrastructure to meet future demands. More importantly, when ITS technologies are deployed, it helps to save lives, time, and money and sustain the environment.

ITS will involve the building of much new system infrastructure and foster demand for many types of terminal equipment, thus it is certain to create a huge market. To take advantage of these promising opportunities, large investments have been made in national projects in Europe, North America and Japan to promote the early realization of ITS.

A flurry of activity is unfolding based on close links among government, industry, and academia. In Europe, ERTICO (ITS Europe, stands for European Road Transport Telematics Implementation Coordination Organization) in the United States, ITS America, in Japan, ITS Japan (former Vehicle, Road and Traffic Intelligence Society (VERTIS)), and other organizations in other countries and areas have been established as parent bodies to promote ITS development. These events reflect a global consensus that ITS will be key to the innovative road transportation systems of the future.

1.2.1 Definition of ITS

There are a number of similar definitions of ITS available from different organizations, which are:

- ITS America (The Intelligent Transportation Society of America): ITS encompass a broad range of information communications and control technologies that improve the safety, efficiency, and performance of the surface transportation system. ITS technologies provide the traveling public with accurate, real-time information, allowing them to make more informed and efficient travel decisions. When integrated into the nation's roadways, vehicles, consumer electronics devices and public transportation networks, ITS can save lives, reduce congestion, improve mobility and optimize the existing infrastructure. ITS investments provide a foundation for long-term benefits including government and industry cost savings, economy-wide productivity improvements, and an improved quality of life.

- IEEE ITSS (The Institute of Electrical and Electronics Engineers ITS Society): ITS are those utilizing synergistic technologies and systems engineering concepts to develop and improve transportation systems of all kinds.

- EU (European Union): ITS are advanced applications which, without embodying intelligence as such, aim to provide innovative services relating to different modes of transport and traffic management and enable various users to be better informed and make safer, more coordinated, and "smarter" use of transport networks.

- ERTICO: ITS are the integration of information and communications technology with transport infrastructure, vehicles and users. By sharing vital information, ITS allow people to get more from transport networks, in greater safety and with less impact on the environment.

- ITS Japan: ITS offer a fundamental solution to various issues concerning transportation, which include traffic accidents, congestion and environmental pollution. ITS deal with these issues through the most advanced communications and control technologies. ITS receive and transmit information on humans, roads and automobiles.

- ITS China (China Intelligent Transportation System Association): ITS are new generation of transportation systems, which are aiming to bring full play the potentials of traffic facilities, improve transport efficiency and service quality, ensure traffic safety, reduce energy consumption and environmental pollution by applying the advanced modern information technology.

By identifying the common references in the above definitions, ITS are such systems that provides the opportunity to integrate travelers, vehicles and infrastructure into comprehensive systems through a range of technologies such as computer science, information technology, communication engineering, automatic controlling, electronics, and system engineering.

Although ITS may refer to all modes of transport, EU defines ITS as systems in which information and communication technologies are applied in the field of road transport, including infrastructure, vehicles and users, and in traffic management and mobility management, as well as for interfaces with other modes of transport.

1.2.2　Mission of ITS

By creating ideal traffic conditions, ITS will reduce traffic accidents and congestion while saving energy and protecting the environment. ITS require not only the roads to be intelligent but variety of transportation, such as railroad, aviation and marine, to cooperate with each other.

The ultimate missions of ITS are:
- zero accidents;
- zero delays;
- reduced impact on the environment;
- fully informed people.

1.2.3　Main Sub-systems of ITS

ITS system could contain many sub-systems. In this section, we shall introduce 5 important sub-systems one by one.

Advanced Transportation Management Systems (ATMS). The ATMS field is a primary subfield within the ITS domain. The ATMS view is a top-down management perspective that integrates technology primarily to improve the flow of vehicle traffic and improve safety. Real-time traffic data from devices on road (e.g. cameras, speed sensors, etc.) flows into a Transportation Management Center (TMC) where these data are integrated and processed (e.g. for incident detection), and may result in actions taken (e.g. traffic routing, Dynamic message signs) with the goal of improving traffic flow.

Advanced Traveler Information Systems (ATIS). ATIS are defined as systems that acquire, analyze, and present information to assist travelers in moving from a starting location (origin) to their desired destination. Information will include location of incidents, weather problems, road conditions, optimal routings, lane restrictions and in-vehicle signing. The information can be provided both to drivers and to interim users, and even to people before a trip to help them decide what mode they should use.

Advanced Vehicle Control Systems (AVCS). AVCS apply additional technology to vehicles to identify obstacles and adjacent vehicles, thereby assist in the prevention of collisions and resulting in safer and more efficient operation at higher speeds. AVCS also may interact with the fully developed ATMS to provide automated vehicle operations.

Advanced Public Transportation Systems (APTS). APTS technologies can help improve transit and ride sharing services. By using global positioning systems (GPS), wireless communication systems, and other devices, passengers are able to get more information about when a bus or carpool will arrive, know where a vehicle is along its route, and purchase a single card or pass that make transfers seamless and automatic. Operators and administrators of these systems are provided better quality information about who is using the services, when, and how.

Commercial Vehicle Operation Systems (CVOS). CVOS select from ATIS those features critical to commercial and emergency vehicles. They expedite deliveries, improve operational efficiency, and increase safety. CVOS are designed to interact with ATMS as both become fully developed. Global competition is changing the way that companies conduct business. Carriers are expected to provide faster, more reliable, and more cost-effective services. CVOS technologies are emerging as a key to reducing costs and improving productivity. Commercial and emergency vehicles will adopt ATIS and link them to ATMS as soon as it is feasible to do so. Additional CVOS technologies (some already have been developed) including weigh-in-motion sensors, automated vehicle-identification transponders, and automated vehicle-classification devices will reduce time spent in weigh stations and labor costs.

1.2.4 ITS Achievements in Hong Kong

To maximize the capacity of the road network and enhance road safety, it is government's objective to encourage the application of new technology to traffic management in Hong Kong. As such, the government has deployed a wide spectrum of advanced technologies in managing traffic and promoted the development and provision of value-added transport services through partnership and collaboration with the private sector, academic and professional institutions. ITS organizations like ITS-HK, a non-profit making learned society established in 2000 to promote the ITS industry among members and to communicate with worldwide ITS organizations, also play an important role in the development of ITS in Hong Kong.

Area Traffic Control Systems. The development of ITS in Hong Kong can be traced back to the time when the first computerized Area Traffic Control (ATC) System in Southeast Asia came to operation in the 1970's.

The ATC System is a computerized system that integrates the control and operation of traffic signals within a district. Since the 1970's, the Transport Department has been expanding the coverage of the ATC systems to all urban areas and new towns in the New Territories. The systems provide better co-ordination of traffic lights at road intersections to help motorists and pedestrians cross roads and junctions safely and efficiently. In March 2012, there are 1821 signalized junctions in the territory of which 1719 are under ATC, with 447 CCTV cameras to monitor the traffic conditions at these junctions.

Automatic Toll Collection System. The Automatic Toll Collection System for road tunnels was first introduced in Hong Kong in 1993. The system was then extended to all tolled tunnels, Lantau Link and Ma Wan Control Area. In March 2012, there are more than 250,000 electronic toll tags issued by the service provider of Automatic Toll Collection System, and about half of the vehicles passing through the tolled tunnels or tolled roads use the system.

Octopus. Launched in September 1997, Octopus is a contactless smart card system jointly developed by the major public transport operators in Hong Kong. It has become very popular and can be used on most of the transport services in Hong Kong including railways, buses, minibuses, coaches, ferries, car parks and parking meters. In addition, Octopus are also accepted for small-value non-transport payments at supermarkets, convenience stores, fast food outlets, cake shops, vending machines and kiosks, household stores, telecommunications, photo booths, cinemas and more. Today, over 25 million cards are in circulation and the number of daily transactions is over 12 million.

Journey Time Indication System. The Journey Time Indication System (JTIS) on Hong Kong Island was commissioned in 2003 to provide the estimated journey time to exit of respective tunnels from Hong Kong Island to Kowloon. The JTIS assists motorists to make an informed route choice to cross the harbor before arriving at the critical diversion points by referring to the journey time information of different cross harbor routes provided by the journey time indicators. A survey conducted in 2006 revealed that the JTIS was welcomed by the public. The Transport Department expanded the JTIS to Kowloon and Eastern District in 2010 to provide motorists with more journey time information to cross the harbor.

The displayed digits on the journey time indicators are shown in three colors for different traffic conditions: Red represents congested traffic, Amber represents slow traffic and Green represents smooth traffic. The JTIS operates on a 24-hour basis and the displayed times are refreshed every two minutes.

1.2.5 The Biggest Event of ITS Society

The ITS World Congress is an annual forum for promoting international cooperation and the presentation of the latest research on ITS. Each year this event is held in different location moving among Europe, the Asia-Pacific region, and North America.

The latest 20th ITS World Congress was held in Tokyo in 2013 and attracted 20,691 participants (including 3,940 registrants) from 65 countries and areas. The 21st and 22nd ITS World Congress will be held in Detroit, Michigan, USA in 2014 and in Bordeaux, France in 2015, respectively.

ERTICO-ITS Europe, ITS America and ITS Japan work closely together in the preparation of this biggest event of ITS society.

1.2.6 Summary

ITS are national level project that will even change the system of society and it has great potential to create new industries and markets.

ITS market is expected to expand rapidly over the next few decades. As a major technological power, we must work to pioneer new business opportunities by engaging in ITS-related research and development needed for constructing new road transport systems, thereby contributing to the well-being of the world.

New Words and Expressions

contemporary [kən'temprərɪ] *adj.* 当代的,现代的

indispensable [ˌɪndɪˈspensəbl]	adj. 不可缺少的，绝对必要的
congest [kənˈdʒest]	vt. 拥挤，拥堵
deteriorate [dɪˈtɪərɪəreɪt]	vt. 使恶化
shrink [ʃrɪŋk]	vt. 收缩
capacity [kəˈpæsətɪ]	n. 容量，才能
	adj. 充其量的，最大限度的
foster [ˈfɔstə(r)]	vt. 培养，促进
consensus [kənˈsensəs]	n. 一致，舆论，合意
innovative [ˈɪnəveɪtɪv]	adj. 革新的，创新的
utilize [ˈjuːtəlaɪz]	vt. 使用，利用
synergistic [ˌsɪnəˈdʒɪstɪk]	adj. 协同的，合作的
various users	各类用户
ultimate [ˈʌltɪmət]	adj. 最后的，极限的，首要的
	n. 极点，顶点
optimal [ˈɔptɪməl]	adj. 最佳的，最优的；最理想的
weigh station	称重站
labor costs	劳动力成本
cross roads and junctions	穿越道路路口
CCTV (Closed Circuit Television)	闭路电视
Automatic Toll Collection System	自动收费系统
fast food outlets	快餐店
estimated journey time	预计行车时间
amber [ˈæmbə(r)]	adj. (交通灯)橙黄色(的)，橘黄色(的)
road transport systems	道路交通系统

Exercises

I. True or false

a) There are a number of similar definitions of ITS available from different organizations.

b) The ultimate missions of ITS are Zero delays.

c) ITS will increase traffic accidents and congestion while saving energy and protecting the environment.

d) The Transport Department has been expanding the coverage of the ATC systems to all urban areas and new towns in the New Territories.

e) The displayed digits on the journey time indicators are shown in three colors for different traffic conditions.

II. Filling blanks

a) The ATC System is a computerized system _____ the control and operation of traffic signals within a district.

b) To maximize the capacity _____ the road network and enhance road safety, it is government's objective to encourage the application of new technology to traffic management in Hong

Kong.

c) ITS _____ with these issues through the most advanced communications and control technologies.

d) ITS market is expected _____ expand rapidly over the next few decades.

e) Operators and administrators of these systems are provided better quality information about _____ is using the services, when, and how.

III. Translation

a) However, a variety of problems—traffic accidents, traffic congestion, environmental pollution, and massive consumption of fossil fuels, to name a few—are becoming serious global problems and critical issues for all humankind. These are issues that require fundamental solutions.

b) ITS offer the concept and approach. In the near future, ITS will arrive that offer fundamental breakthroughs in safety, congestion reduction, driving comfort, and environmental friendliness, bringing them to levels far higher than those provided by current road transportation systems.

c) ITS, standing for either intelligent transportation systems or intelligent transport systems, offer the concept and approach. ITS technologies enable us to make better use of the transportation network we already have while building smarter infrastructure to meet future demands. More importantly, when ITS technologies are deployed, it helps to save lives, time, and money and sustain the environment.

1.3 Call for Papers IEEE-ITSC2013

The IEEE Conference on Intelligent Transportation Systems is the annual flagship conference of the IEEE Intelligent Transportation Systems Society. IEEE-ITSC 2013 welcomes articles in the field of Intelligent Transportation Systems, conveying new developments in theory, analytical and numerical simulation and modeling, experimentation, advanced deployment and case studies, results of laboratory or field operational test.

The theme of the IEEE-ITSC 2013 conference is Intelligent Transportation Systems for All Transportation Modes. Major advances in information and communication technology are enabling a vast array of new possibilities in transportation.

ITS are emerging worldwide to make transportation more efficient, reliable, cleaner and safer. ITS are used in road, water, rail and air transportation to collect information about transportation flows from a multitude of sources and manage them effectively, shifting collective traffic and transportation management paradigms towards end user orientation.

1.3.1 Program Topics

The technical areas include but are not limited to the following:
- Multi-modal ITS
- Advanced Public Transportation Management
- Ports, Waterways, Inland navigation, and Vessel Traffic Management
- Modeling, Simulation, and Control of Pedestrians and Cyclists

- Air, Road, and Rail Traffic Management
- ITS User services
- Emergency Management
- Transportation Networks
- Emissions, Noise, Environment
- Management of Exceptional Events: Incidents, Evacuation, Emergency Management
- Security Systems
- Safety Systems
- Driver and Traveler Support Systems
- Commercial Vehicle Operations
- Intelligent logistics
- Sensing and Intervening, Detectors and Actuators
- Data Management Systems
- Communication in ITS
- Cooperative Techniques and Systems
- Intelligent Vehicles
- Vision, and Environment Perception
- Electric Vehicle Transportation Systems
- Electronic Payment Systems
- Intelligent Techniques in ITS
- Traffic Theory for ITS
- Modeling, Control and Simulation
- Human Factors, Travel Behavior
- ITS Field Tests and Implementation

1.3.2 Organizing Committee

General Chair: Bart van Arem
General Co-Chair: Hans van Lint
Program Chair: Andreas Hegyi
Program Co-Chair: Bart De Schutter
Special Sessions Chair: Alfredo Nunez
Special Sessions Co-Chair: Hans van Lint
Finance Chair: Felicita Viglietti
Publications, Publicity, and Sponsoring Chair: Vincent Marchau
Local Arrangements and Registration Chair: Nicole Fontein

1.3.3 Important Dates

Special session proposal submission deadline: February 25, 2013
Full paper submission deadline: March 15, 2013
Workshop/tutorial proposal submission deadline: May 1, 2013

Notification of acceptance: June 1, 2013

Final paper submission deadline: August 7, 2013 (FINAL Extension)

Conference date: October 6-9, 2013

1.3.4 Venue

Steigenberger Kurhaus Hotel, HAGUE, Netherlands.

The Steigenberger Kurhaus Hotel in Scheveningen is more than just a hotel: it is a national landmark of the Netherlands. This 5-star hotel with its characteristic facade combines modern comfort with an atmospheric, historic ambience. Leisure seekers as well as those on business, participating in a meeting or conference, will certainly encounter a hotel with style.

Experience the culture of times gone by, characterized with style, luxury and service to a high standard. Enjoy the sea, ambience, culinary delights as well as everything else the Steigenberger Kurhaus Hotel has to offer.

In summer guests can also enjoy a seat on the most beautiful outdoor cafe of the entire North Sea coast.

1.3.5 Paper Submission

Complete manuscripts in PDF format must be electronically submitted for peer-review in IEEE standard format. Detailed submission instructions can be found through the conference website.

1.3.6 Special Sessions

Special session organization is encouraged. Proposals for workshops, tutorials, and special sessions should be submitted via the conference submission website.

1.3.7 Awards

A "Best Paper Award" and a "Best Student Paper Award" will be conferred to the author(s) of a full paper presented at the conference, selected by the Awards Committee.

The "Best Student Paper Award" will be given to a paper of which the first author is a student.

All reviewed papers are eligible for the "Best Paper Award" (regular papers and special session papers), except the ones that have been nominated for the "Best Student Paper Award". No nomination is necessary for the "Best Paper Award".

1.3.8 Journal and Magazine Publication of Selected Papers

Selected papers of exceptional quality will be invited for submission to a special issue of the IEEE Transactions on Intelligent Transportation Systems or the IEEE Intelligent Transportation Systems Magazine. Authors will be asked to revise their papers according to the standards of the Transactions or the Magazine. The papers will be subject to the Transactions' and Magazine's review process.

1.3.9 Who Should Attend

Those in ITS research, development, design, deployment, planning, and decision making who are in academic institutions, transportation industry, automotive manufacturers and suppliers, government, local transport authorities, national labs, international organizations, public transport authorities, freight and transport operators, public transport operators, service providers, telecom operators, system integrators, commercial fleet owners, road operators, and motoring organizations and all others who are in the energy and environment sector with an interest in transportation systems will benefit by attending this unique conference.

1.3.10 Conference Website

http://ieee-itsc13.org/

New Words and Expressions

flagship ['flægʃɪp]	n. 旗舰;最重要的一个;佼佼者
in the field of	在……领域
convey [kən'veɪ]	vt. 传送,输送
simulation [ˌsɪmju'leɪʃn]	n. 模仿,模拟,假装,装病
experimentation [ɪkˌsperɪmen'teɪʃn]	n. 实验,试验;实验法
a vast array of	大量的
emerge [ɪ'mɜːdʒ]	vi. 出现,浮现,暴露,摆脱
multitude ['mʌltɪtjuːd]	n. 大量,许多
navigation [ˌnævɪ'geɪʃn]	n. 航行(学),航海(术)
vessel ['vesl]	n. 容器;船,飞船;血管,管束
rail [reɪl]	n. 轨道,钢轨;扶手
evacuation [ɪˌvækju'eɪʃn]	n. 撤空;撤离;撤退;疏散
facade [fə'sɑːd]	n. 表象;虚伪,假象
comfort ['kʌmfət]	n. 舒适,安慰,慰藉
ambience ['æmbɪəns]	n. 气氛,布景;周围环境;
encounter [ɪn'kaʊntə(r)]	n. 碰见;遭遇战;对决,冲突
culinary ['kʌlɪnərɪ]	adj. 烹调用的
award [ə'wɔːd]	n. 奖品;法院、(法官的)判决;裁定书
nominate ['nɒmɪneɪt]	v. 提名,推荐,任命

Exercises

Ⅰ. True or false

a) Special session proposal submission deadline: February 25, 2013.

b) Major advances in information and communication technology are enabling a vast array of new possibilities in transportation.

c) Complete manuscripts in DOC format must be electronically submitted for peer-review in

IEEE standard format.

d) The "Best Student Paper Award" will be given to a paper of which the author is a student.

e) All accepted papers will be invited for submission to a special issue of the IEEE Transactions on Intelligent Transportation Systems or the IEEE Intelligent Transportation Systems Magazine.

II. Filling blanks

a) IEEE-ITSC 2013 welcomes articles _____ of Intelligent Transportation Systems.

b) Those in ITS research, development, design, deployment, planning, and decision making will benefit by _____ this unique conference.

c) The IEEE Conference on Intelligent Transportation Systems is the _____ flagship conference of the IEEE Intelligent Transportation Systems Society.

d) _____ papers of exceptional quality will be invited for submission to journals.

e) The papers will be _____ to the Transactions' and Magazine's review process.

III. Translation

a) Those in ITS research, development, design, deployment, planning, and decision making who are in academic institutions, transportation industry, automotive manufacturers and suppliers, government, local transport authorities, national labs, international organizations, public transport authorities, freight and transport operators, public transport operators, service providers, telecom operators, system integrators, commercial fleet owners, road operators, and motoring organizations and all others who are in the energy and environment sector with an interest in transportation systems will benefit by attending this unique conference.

b) The theme of the IEEE-ITSC 2013 conference is Intelligent Transportation Systems for All Transportation Modes. Major advances in information and communication technology are enabling a vast array of new possibilities in transportation.

c) Complete manuscripts in PDF format must be electronically submitted for peer-review in IEEE standard format. Detailed submission instructions can be found through the conference website.

Chapter 2 Advanced Transportation Management Systems (ATMS)

2.1 Sensing Traffic Using Sensors

There are a number of ways to detect vehicles, ranging from ultra-sonic to inductive loop. For traffic control or drive-thru, inductive loop technology is the most reliable, bar none.

An inductive loop vehicle detector system (Figure 2.1) consists of three components: a loop (preformed or saw-cut), loop extension cable and a detector. When installing or repairing an inductive loop system the smallest detail can mean the difference between reliable detection and an intermittent detection of vehicles. Therefore, attention to detail when installing or troubleshooting an inductive loop vehicle detection system is absolutely critical.

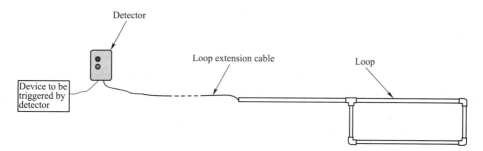

Figure 2.1 The loop vehicle detector system

2.1.1 How It Works

The preformed or saw-cut loop is buried in the traffic lane. The loop is a continuous run of wire that enters and exits from the same point. The two ends of the loop wire are connected to the loop extension cable, which in turn connects to the vehicle detector. The detector powers the loop causing a magnetic field in the loop area. The loop resonates at a constant frequency that the detector monitors. A base frequency is established when there is no vehicle over the loop. When a large metal object, such as a vehicle, moves over the loop, the resonate frequency increases. This increase in frequency is sensed and, depending on the design of the detector, forces a normally open relay to close. The relay will remain closed until the vehicle leaves the loop and the frequency returns to the base level. The relay can trigger any number of devices such as an audio intercom system, a gate, a traffic light, etc.

In general, a compact car will cause a greater increase in frequency than a full size car or truck. This occurs because the metal surfaces on the under carriage of the vehicle are closer to the loop. Figures 2.2 illustrates how the under carriage of a sports car is well within the magnetic field of the loop compared to the sports utility vehicle. Notice that the frequency change is greater with the smaller vehicle.

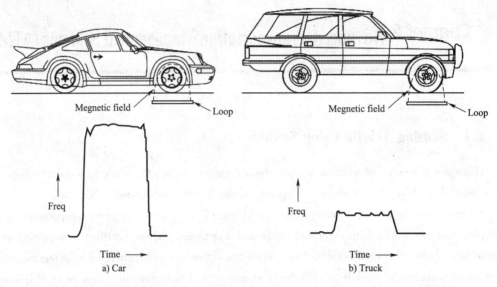

Figure 2.2 The relationship of frequency and time

Also, it is interesting to note that the frequency change is very consistent between two vehicles of the same make and model, so much so that a detector can almost be designed to determine the type of vehicle over the loop.

There is a misconception that inductive loop vehicle detection is based on metal mass. This is simply not true. Detection is based on metal surface area, otherwise known as skin effect. The greater the surface area of metal in the same plane as the loop, the greater the increase in frequency. For example, a one square foot piece of sheet metal positioned in the same plane of the loop has the same affect as a hunk of metal one foot square and one foot thick. Another way to illustrate the point is to take the same one square foot piece of sheet metal, which is easily detected (Figure 2.3a)) when held in the same plane as the loop, and turn it perpendicular to the loop and it becomes impossible to detect (Figure 2.3b)). Keep this principle in mind when dealing with inductive loop detectors.

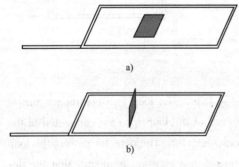

Figure 2.3 1' sq sheet metal in plane of loop
a) Easily detected; b) Not detectable

2.1.2 Preformed and Saw-cut Loops

A preformed loop is typically 3 to 5 turns of loop wire encased in PVC pipe for use in new construction before the pavement is installed (Figure 2.4). The loop wire is 14 or 16 awg stranded machine tool wire with an insulation of XLPE (cross-linked polyethylene) encased in PVC pipe to hold the loop's shape and to protect the loop wire from damage while the pavement is installed.

A saw-cut loop is used when the pavement is already in place. The installation involves cutting the loop shape in the pavement with a concrete saw, laying the loop wire in the slot, pressing in a polyfoam backward to keep the wire compacted and finishing with saw-cut loop sealant or street bond to fill the slot and protect the wire (Figure 2.5).

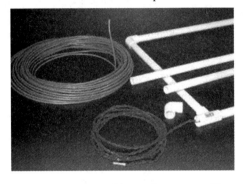 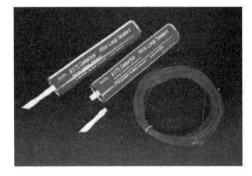

Figure 2.4   Preformed loop with extension cable   Figure 2.5   Saw-cut loop kit with wire and loop sealant

It is best to use the recommended 14 or 16-awg machine tool wire for loop installation. The insulation has a high resistance to water, heat, abrasions, oils and gasoline. Purchase the wire from the same source you bought the saw-cut loop sealant to be sure to get the correct wire.

1) Loop Extension Cable

Loop extension cable is used to extend the distance from the preformed or saw-cut loop to the vehicle detector, which is usually located indoors or in a weatherproof enclosure. The characteristics of the extension cable are just as important as the characteristics of the loop wire. Use only 14, 16, or 18 awg stranded 2 conductor twisted, shielded cable with a polyethylene insulation jacket. The extension cable connections to the loop wire and the vehicle detector wires must be soldered. Do not use any other method for connection. The distance between the loop and the detector can safely be extended to 300 feet with proper extension cable, however check with the vehicle detector manufacturer for confirmation.

2) Loop Vehicle Detector

The proper installation and material is critical! In general, loop vehicle detectors from all manufacturers work under the same principle and will all work reliably if the installation is done properly and the correct materials are used.

Vehicle detector features differ between manufacturers, and most are straight forward. The following features need special consideration.

• Number of Outputs. Most detectors provide a switch closure via a relay, which is typically configured as normally open. It is the number of outputs provided that may be important and how they can be configured. More and more devices, particularly in the drive-thru environments, need to be triggered by vehicle detection, such as audio communication, car timing, message greeting, electronic menu boards, gates, etc. Determine the number of devices that will be used now and in the future with the vehicle detector and match or exceed that number with the number of available relay outputs.

• Signal Type. All detectors provide a constant presence style of signal output. In other words, the relay output is closed the entire time that a vehicle is present over the loop, and does not open again until the vehicle drives away. Most devices require this style of output signal, however some devices require a pulse style, which will only momentarily close the relay at the time when the vehicle is detected. Check the requirements of the devices that you are connecting to the detector. If you are connecting more than one device to the detector, make sure that the detector can provide the required signal types at the same time. Some detectors can only provide one or the other style of signal output at a time.

• Diagnostics. Some detectors provide PC diagnostics via a communication port on the detector. Diagnostic software gives you a visual picture of what is happening at the loop, and will help you troubleshoot any problems you may experience during installation or in the future. Detectors with this feature are usually in the same price range as other detectors and can help you save time solving a detection problem. The PC software and cable is usually additional (Figure 2.6), however keep in mind that if you have multiple installations you need only buy the software and cable setup once. Diagnostics software can also help determine the depth and position of the loop in the pavement.

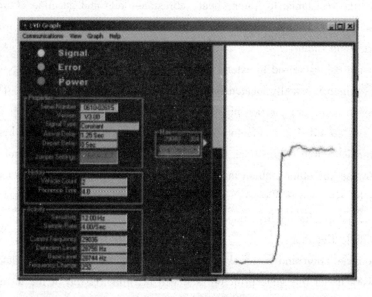

Figure 2.6   Screen shot of diagnostics software

2.1.3 Location

Location, Location, Location! The position of the loop relative to the vehicles you are trying to detect is extremely important. Vehicles entering a fast food restaurant drive-thru lane will stop at the menu board with the driver's window positioned in line with the speaker post. The front axle is the only metal surface whose relative position to the driver is consistent from vehicle to vehicle (Figure 2.7). Because of this fact, the vehicle detector is designed to pick up the front axle, not the vehicle's engine. Therefore, the loop should be positioned 1 1/2 to 2 feet ahead of the speaker post, with the long axis of the loop running perpendicular to the traffic lane. This positions the axle of the vehicle directly over the loop in the same direction as the loop.

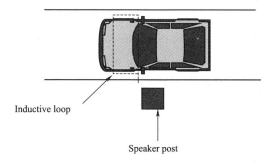

Figure 2.7 Proper location of loop to pick up metal of front axle

The proper installation and location of the loop are the most important aspects of reliable vehicle detection. In recent years, there has been an increase in the number of missed and false detections due to the popularity of SUVs. The missed detections can be attributed to two factors. First, an most obvious, is that the metal surface area of the taller vehicles is farther away from the loop which makes the vehicle more difficult to detect. Second, and less obvious, is that larger vehicles have a greater turning radius. The driver finds it difficult in some drive-thru lanes to round the corner prior to the loop and as a result, the vehicle becomes positioned further away from the curb and not properly positioned over the loop (Figure 2.8). Compound the poor position of the vehicle with the height of the vehicle and you have a difficult vehicle to detect.

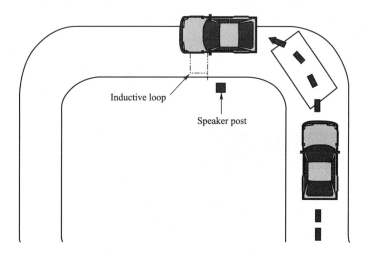

Figure 2.8 Drive-thru showing tight traffic lane

1) Loop Installation

Follow closely the manufacturers installation instructions for the saw-cut or preformed loop that you purchased. However, there are a couple of important points to make with regard to saw-cut loop and preformed loop installation.

It is important that when the installation is complete the loop be no more than 2″ below the surface of the asphalt or concrete. The deeper the loop the less sensitive the loop detection system becomes.

It is also important that the lead-in wires from the detector to the beginning of the loop be twisted a minimum of five times per foot.

2) Saw-cut Loop Installation

When installing a saw-cut loop inspect the cable for any nicks in the protective jacket. Reject and replace any nicked wire. Never splice the loop wire except to splice the loop extension cable to the loop lead in wires and to splice the vehicle detector lead wires to the extension cable. Always solder the connections, never use a short cut such as wire nuts (Figure 2.9).

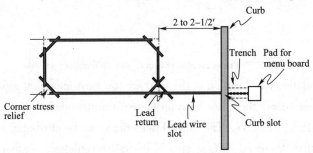

Figure 2.9   The example of installing loop

When making the loop pattern with a concrete saw, cut the corners of the rectangle at a 45-degree angle. This reduces stress and the possibility of nicking the wire outer jacket.

Always use backer rod pressed into the saw-cuts to secure the loop wire before using the street sealer. If backer rod is not used the loop wire will float in the saw-cut slot while the street sealer is curing, resulting in air pockets (Figure 2.10). If air pockets exist, the loop wire will move whenever the pavement vibrates and false detections will occur.

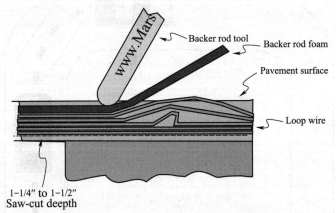

Figure 2.10   The installation of the loop wire

3) Preformed Loop Installation

Preparation of the loop area prior to placing the loop is important. Start by cutting back any and all concrete reinforcement such as rebar at least 2' from the outer parameter of the loop. Rebar will reduce the sensitivity of the detector (Figure 2.11). Most detectors are designed to tune out rebar, but rebar will decrease the sensitivity, so take the time now to avoid a problem later.

Next place the preformed loop onto stakes in order to position the loop 2" below the finished surface (Figure 2.12).

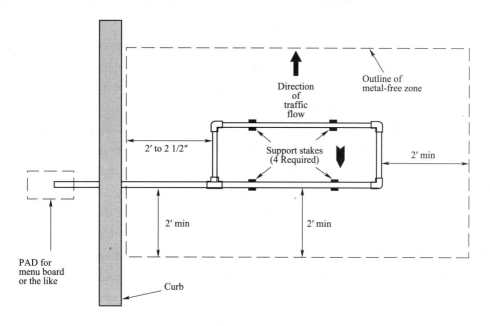

Figure 2.11 Preformed loop installation

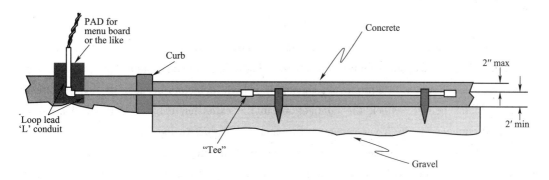

Figure 2.12 Vertical section of the loop installation

2.1.4 Sensitivity

Most vehicle detectors have adjustable settings for sensitivity. If the detector is missing vehicles then the sensitivity is set too low. If the detector is jumpy or is creating false detections, it may be set too sensitive. However, all inductive loop detectors are dealing with the same physical characteristics of a magnetic field in a loop. The maximum height of detection is roughly 2/3 the length of the short side of the loop. For example, if you have a loop that is $18'' \times 60''$, the maximum height of detection is $12''$ from the loop. Most manufacturers have managed to push the height of detection to the full length of the short side, however keep in mind this is not as reliable.

The most effective way to increase sensitivity is to lengthen the short side of the loop. Most drive-thru loops are 18 to 24 inches wide. If you take an $18'' \times 60''$ loop and increase the short side to $24''$, you have increased the height of detection by $4''$. However, making the loop too wide can cause a different problem. In the drive-thru scenario where vehicles move slowly, and bumper to bumper, a system that is too sensitive may not be able to identify the gap between vehicles causing a missed detection.

Another misconception about loop sensitivity is that increasing the number of turns in the loop will increase sensitivity. Increasing or decreasing the number of turns does not affect sensitivity. Increasing the number of turns increases stability. Three to five turns is ideal for maintaining the proper stability and sensitivity combination.

The frequency of the loop will change as the environment changes, as a result most detectors are designed to constantly adjust to this slow change in frequency over time. The detector's purpose is to detect rapid changes in frequency. However, inductive loops and detectors are sensitive to temperature. When the temperature of the inductive loop increases, the frequency will decrease, and the opposite is true of the detector. When the temperature of the detector increases the frequency will increase. If the temperature of either the loop or the detector increases or decreases too fast, false detections will occur. The loop, buried in the pavement is not likely to change temperature rapidly, however mounting the detector in the wrong place can cause such a problem. For example, mounting the detector directly in line with a window where it can get a cold blast of air whenever the window is open, can result in problems.

2.1.5 Troubleshooting

Most detectors provide LEDs that will indicate a problem with the loop, such as a short or an open. It is possible for a problem to occur that will cause the error indicating LED to stay on and yet the installation is ok, but simply needs a reset. Lightning can cause such a problem. Electrical storms can cause havoc with equipment, especially vehicle detectors because the loop is outside.

If problems persist, check the connections to the extension cable and to the loop lead-in wires. Bad connections are a very common problem with inductive loops.

If the installed detector has a communications port for diagnostics, beg, borrow or steal, a copy of the software and cabling needed to utilize this feature. Diagnostics software is an amazingly powerful tool for diagnostics, is less expensive than the test equipment needed to do the same job and will provide more information. Some diagnostics software will even capture the data to disk. This is especially useful if you have an intermittent problem. You can leave the computer running for days in order to capture the problem.

In addition to using diagnostics software to capture or see a problem as it occurs it can often be used to help locate the loop in the pavement in order to determine if it's been properly positioned and buried at the right depth.

If a communications port is not available, the next best thing is a megaohm meter. After disconnecting the loop from the detector, place one lead of the meter to one of the lead wires of the loop and the other to earth ground. The resistance should be greater than 100 megaohms. If the resistance is between 50 and 100 megaohms then it is possible that the loop wire is nicked or the extension cable has been damaged. If the resistance is less than 50 megaohms, the loop is shorted to ground. In either case the loop or the extension cable must be replaced.

2.1.6 Summary

Inductive loop detection is relatively simple as a system, but it is important to arm yourself with the knowledge of how it works and how the pieces interrelate. There is no question that a problematic installation can be extremely frustrating, but if you break it down to basics it can be solved more efficiently.

Notes:
- Use a preformed loop before pavement is installed.
- Use a saw-cut loop when pavement has already been installed.
- The loop should be buried no more than 2″ below the asphalt or concrete surface.
- Replace any loop wire that has nicks or splices in the insulation.
- Loop wire should be 14 or 16 awg machine tool wire with XLPE insulation.
- Loops should be no less than three turns and no greater than five.
- The number of turns increases stability of the signal over long runs between the loop and detector.
- The number of turns does not affect sensitivity.
- Extension cable should be 14, 16, or 18 awg twisted/shielded 2-conductor cable with polyethylene jacket.
- The wires that lead into the loop must be twisted a minimum of five turns per foot.
- The maximum height of detection is roughly 2/3 the length of the short side of the loop.
- Connections to the detector, the loop and the extension cable should be soldered.
- The frequency decreases as the temperature of the loop increases.
- The frequency increases as the temperature of the detector increases.

New Words and Expressions

inductive [ɪnˈdʌktɪv]	adj. [数] 归纳的;[电] 感应的
bar none	绝无仅有,没有例外,毫无例外
frequency [ˈfriːkwənsɪ]	n. 频率;频繁
loop [luːp]	v. 使成环;以环连接;使翻筋斗
	n. 环;圈;弯曲部分;翻筋斗
perpendicular [ˌpɜː(r)pənˈdɪkjʊlə(r)]	adj. 垂直的;直立的;陡峭的
	n. 垂线
preformed [ˈpriːˈfɔːmd]	adj. 预成型的;预制成的
polyfoam [ˈpɑlɪfəʊm]	n. 泡沫塑料
confirmation [ˌkɑnfə(r)ˈmeɪʃ(ə)n]	n. 确认;证实
reliably [rɪˈlaɪəblɪ]	adv. 可靠地;确实地
trigger [ˈtrɪgə(r)]	v. 引发;引起;触发
	n. 扳机
style [staɪl]	n. 风格;时尚
	v. 设计

software ['sɒf(t)ˌweə(r)]	n. 软件
positioned [pə'zɪʃ(ə)n]	n. 位置;方位
	v. 安置;把……放在适当位置
attribute ['ætrɪˌbjut]	n. 属性;特质
	v. 归属;把……归于
installation [ˌɪnstə'leɪʃ(ə)n]	n. 安装;装置
minimum ['mɪnɪməm]	n. 最小值;最低限度
	adj. 最小的
occur [ə'kɜː(r)]	v. 发生;出现;存在
reinforcement [ˌriːɪn'fɔː(r)smənt]	n. 加固;增援
roughly ['rʌflɪ]	adv. 粗糙地;概略地
combination [ˌkɒmbɪ'neɪʃ(ə)n]	n. 结合;组合
sensitive ['sensətɪv]	adj. 敏感的;感觉的
	n. 敏感的人;有灵异能力的人
capture ['kæptʃə(r)]	v. 俘获;夺得
	n. 捕获;战利品;俘虏

Exercises

I. True or false

a) When installing or repairing an inductive loop system the smallest detail can mean the difference between reliable detection and an intermittent detection of vehicles.

b) In general, a compact car will cause a greater increase in frequency than a full size car or truck. This occurs because the Plastic material on the under carriage of the vehicle are closer to the loop.

c) Loop extension cable is used to extend the distance from the preformed or saw-cut loop to the vehicle detector, which is usually located outdoors or in a anti-oxidation enclosure.

d) The proper installation and location of the loop are the most important aspects of reliable vehicle detection. In recent years, there has been an increase in the number of missed and false detections due to the popularity of SUVs.

e) The frequency of the loop will change as the temperature changes, as a result most detectors are designed to constantly adjust to this slow change in frequency over time.

II. Filling blanks

a) Also, it is interesting to note that the frequency change is very consistent _____ two vehicles of the same make and model, so much so that a detector can almost be designed to determine the type of vehicle over the loop.

b) _____ the number of devices that will be used now and in the future with the vehicle detector and match or exceed that number with the number of available relay outputs.

c) Most detectors are designed to tune out rebar, but rebar will _____ the sensitivity, so take the time now to avoid a problem later.

d) When making the loop pattern with a concrete saw, cut the corners of the rectangle at a

45-degree angle. This _____ stress and the possibility of nicking the wire outer jacket.

e) In addition to using diagnostics software to capture or see a problem as it occurs it can often be used to help locate the loop in the pavement in order to _____ if it's been properly positioned and buried at the right depth.

III. Translation

a) There are a number of ways to detect vehicles, ranging from ultra-sonic to inductive loop. For traffic control or drive-thru, inductive loop technology is the most reliable, bar none.

b) The missed detections can be attributed to two factors. First, an most obvious, is that the metal surface area of the taller vehicles is farther away from the loop which makes the vehicle more difficult to detect. Second, and less obvious, is that larger vehicles have a greater turning radius.

c) Inductive loop detection is relatively simple as a system, but it is important to arm yourself with the knowledge of how it works and how the pieces interrelate. There is no question that a problematic installation can be extremely frustrating, but if you break it down to basics it can be solved more efficiently.

2.2 Traffic Surveillance and Management

Traffic control is an outdoors occupation, night or day for long hours in all weathers, and is considered a dangerous occupation due to the high risk of being struck by passing vehicles. Safety equipment is vitally important. Fatigue is a big issue, as tired TC's may forget to watch their traffic, or may inadvertently turn their "Stop bats" to the "Slow" position. Many drivers are annoyed by the disruption to their route, and some are sufficiently antisocial as to aim at traffic controllers. Other drivers simply don't pay enough attention to the road, often from using their mobile (cell-) phones, or because they are tired from a night shift at work. Not a few are exceeding the posted speed limit.

Typically, a worksite will be set up with warning signage well in advance of the actual work area. This may involve (in Australia) "Roadworks Ahead", temporary speed restrictions, "Worker Symbolic" (a stylised workman with a pile of rubble, black silhouette on a retrospective orange background), "Reduce Speed", "Lane Status" boards (indicating that some lanes on a multilane will be closed), "Prepare to Stop" and advisory signs telling what's happening (e.g. Water Over Road, Trucks Entering, and Power Line Works Ahead). If lanes have been closed, large flashing arrows (arrow-boards) on trailers may be utilized to give motorists hundreds of meters warning to move over. Motorists will be advised they are leaving a worksite by speed reinstatement or "End Roadworks" signs.

The worksite will usually involve reserving a part of the road for the work area. How this is done depends on the type of road: on a multi-lane road, one or more lanes will be closed off and traffic merged into the remaining lane(s), using cones and "Chevron" signs and arrow-boards to guide motorists. On a wide road (more than 3 meters per lane in Australia), traffic could be "diverted" around the work area by using cones to define a new road centerline and another line of cones around the work area. Sometimes, it is necessary to close a road and detour traffic.

Often, the road is not wide enough to permit opposing streams of traffic past the work area.

Then it is necessary to use "Stop/Slow", where each stream is allowed past the work area in turn. On an intersection, this may involve four or more streams. At signalized intersections, it may be necessary to have the traffic lights disabled.

Sometimes on dual carriageways, it is necessary to divert one carriageway onto the opposing carriageway, forming a "contraflow". This cannot be done "on the fly", as high-speed (100 + km/h), high-volume (500 - 1000 + vehicles per hour) traffic is involved, generating a huge risk to workers. In this case advisory signs will be erected weeks or even months in advance, and new lanes defined by bollards anchored firmly to the road-base will be installed, usually at night when traffic is expected to be minimal. Programmable Variable Message Boards may be utilized at strategic locations to inform motorists. Such "contraflow" situations also pose significant risk to pedestrians who may not be alert to traffic coming from the wrong direction.

2.2.1 Australia

• Sydney. Traffic control is governed by the Australian Standard AS 1742.3-2009, and by State variations. Risk management is regulated under Australian/New Zealand Standard. Traffic controllers are required to wear high-visibility clothing which meets the Australian Standard Australian/New Zealand Standard.

Personal safety is emphasized in all Australian training. This ranges from proper clothing to learning appropriate behavior (for example, always face oncoming traffic). Clothing is considered part of PPE—Personal Protective Equipment—which includes steel-capped boots, sunscreen, broad-brim hats, gloves and sunglasses.

The traffic control process usually starts with a traffic control plan (traffic control plan). A traffic control crew may consist of one person running a simple diversion or closure of a cul-de-sac, up to multiple two- or three-person crews for a complex task. One example of such a complex task is the transport of very wide loads taking all available road space, over several kilometers, usually on an arterial road or highway. In these cases, the affected roads can be closed or contraflowed for the entire day, creating enormous disruption to motorists. Management of the event involves monitoring and closing all intersections, Stop/Slow to work traffic streams through partially closed intersections, and detours. The amount of signage required can be staggering, needing some hours to put in place. Normally a single two-person crew with one tool is sufficient for most jobs.

Not all TC's are employed by dedicated traffic management companies. Many construction companies and government authorities employ their own traffic management. In these cases, TC's will work in other capacities when traffic management is not required.

Traffic control is generally not seen as a career for young people, but rather as a stop-gap while something better is sought. However, older people are often valued by employers for their life-experience, and find that the relatively light manual tool compensates for the discomforts and rigours of the job. There is a career path, but it is dictated by one's own ability and willingness to work.

• Western Australia. Cone taper for a "slow lane" closure showing small chevron (shifter), 40 km/h repeater, chevron and arrow-board.

Accreditation course standards and variations to the Australian Standards are regulated by Main Roads Western Australia (MRWA), part of the Ministry of Planning and Infrastructure.

In Western Australia, use of the Stop/Slow bat is authorized under Regulation 83 of the Road Traffic Code 2000—it is an offence to disobey a traffic controller's bat, punishable by 3 demerit points and 3 penalty units (about $175). Other States have similar provisions.

Traffic controllers must be accredited in Basic Worksite Traffic Management BCC3028A and the Worksite Traffic Controller Course BCC1014A. These qualifications must be renewed after three years, and a refresher course is necessary. The courses take about 4 hours each, and are designed as inductions to on-the-job training.

The Advanced Worksite Traffic Management (AWTM) requires two years experience as a qualified TC as a minimum prerequisite, and must also be renewed after three years. Roadworks Traffic Managers can be accredited with a minimum of five years experience, current "Road Safety Auditor" accreditation and current AWTM accreditation. This qualification is also valid for three years.

All employers require drug screening at least annually and often randomly; many employers such as Australia's leading traffic management company Triaxion Traffic Management and many others require daily blood/alcohol tests; some require police clearance checks. Zero-tolerance is universal. Traffic controllers are usually employed on a casual basis, with wages around $16 to $25 per hour.

2.2.2 Canada

- British Columbia. In BC, Work Safe BC regulates the training of Traffic Control Persons (TCPS), stating that TCPs must be trained in a manner acceptable to the Board. This ensures a high level of training for this high-risk occupation. Currently, the only acceptable course in the province is a two-day session which includes theory and practical components. Royal Canadian Mounted Police (RCMP) Superintendent Derek Cooke of Langley believes that the RCMP should not perform the function of road traffic control to cater to events in support of for-profit corporations unless the municipal government has coordinated or is in support of the event.
- Nova Scotia. In Nova Scotia training is regulated by the Nova Scotia Department of Transportation and Infrastructure Renewal. There is a one-day course for TCPS and a two-day course for Temporary Workplace Signers. Signers are responsible for the setup of signs, cones etc., and making sure the setup complies with the NS Temporary Workplace Traffic Control Manual
- Newfoundland & Labrador (NL). All flag persons-or traffic control persons (TCP)-in Newfoundland and Labrador are now required to complete a TCP training course approved by the Workplace Health, Safety and Compensation Commission.

Proper traffic control is critical for the safety of workers, drivers and the general public. Without training by a Commission approved training provider, workers are not permitted to work as a TCP on our province's roads.

The Commission's Traffic Control Person (TCP) Certification Training Standard establishes criteria for TCP training providers and trainers.

TCP training providers must apply and be approved by the Commission to deliver TCP certification training.

The delivery of training prepares the TCP to perform traffic control in a safe and competent manner by providing them with the knowledge and skills to work safely, consistent with industry and legislative standards.

Traffic Control Person (TCP) Certification Training has an expiry date of 3 years, upon which the course must be completed again for renewal.

2.2.3 United States

Although the Federal Highway Administration specifies standards and guidelines through the MUTCD which apply to the usage of traffic control equipment, individual state and local agencies can provide variations or additions to these standards.

The transportation system in the United States is complex and extensive. Traffic volumes, types of vehicles, driving styles, population density, speed limits, and many other factors vary dramatically from one region to the next. As a result, highway traffic control measures (including type of equipment and implementation), are not strictly consistent. Federal Guidelines do not address certification methods for traffic controllers, flaggers, or other personnel responsible for traffic control. This responsibility is managed on a state or local agency level, and therefore certification requirements are not consistent and are administered locally. Safety standards (irrespective of traffic control) are mandated by OSHA as well as state-level occupational safety departments.

A construction traffic control company operates in the same basic way as any other construction company. Companies submit a bid for a job, the lowest bid is accepted (except in the case of disadvantaged companies), and the labor is provided to the contractor or agency in charge. Typically speaking, flaggers work in groups of 5 to 10 under a TCS, or Traffic Control Supervisor. The TCS is responsible for placing the flaggers correctly, ensuring that they receive the proper breaks and supervision, and placing the cautionary signs (such as Road Work Ahead, One Lane Road Ahead, and Uneven Lanes). Flaggers is the second line of attention for drivers. They are the first people in the work zone to deal with opposing traffic. It is one of the most responsible jobs in traffic control.

While construction traffic control in the U.S. used to be a widely unionized profession, it is now dominated by private business and wages are not controlled by the union.

2.2.4 United Kingdom

Traffic management in Scotland is handled by Traffic Scotland and Transport Scotland. In Scotland, as in the rest of the UK, the most iconic image of a traffic controller is in the form of a "lollipop man" or "lollipop woman" who aids children in road crossing on their journey to school.

New Words and Expressions

surveillance[sə(r)'veɪləns]　　　　　　　　　n. 监督；监视
occupation[ˌɒkjʊ'peɪʃ(ə)n]　　　　　　　　n. 职业；占有；消遣

annoy [əˈnɔɪ]		v. 骚扰;惹恼
		n. 烦恼(等于 annoyance)
exceed [ɪkˈsiːd]		v. 超过;胜过
involve [ɪnˈvɒlv]		v. 包含;牵涉
contraflow [ˈkɒntrəˌfləʊ]		n. 反向流动;逆流
staggering [ˈstæɡərɪŋ]		adj. 蹒跚的;令人惊愕的;犹豫的
		v. 蹒跚(stagger 的 ing 形式)
sufficient [səˈfɪʃ(ə)nt]		adj. 足够的;充分的
discomfort [dɪsˈkʌmfə(r)t]		n. 不适;不安;不便之处
		v. 使……不舒服;使……不安
authorise [ˈɔːθəraɪz]		v. 授权;批准;委任
accredit [əˈkredɪt]		v. 授权;信任;归因于
renew [rɪˈnjuː]		v. 使更新;续借
qualification [ˌkwɒlɪfɪˈkeɪʃ(ə)n]		n. 资格;条件;限制
acceptable [əkˈseptəb(ə)l]		adj. 可接受的;合意的
course [kɔː(r)s]		n. 科目;课程
		v. 追赶;跑过
approve [əˈpruːv]		v. 批准;为……提供证据
certification [ˌsɜːtɪfɪˈkeɪʃn]		n. 证明;保证;检定
delivery [dɪˈlɪv(ə)rɪ]		n. [贸易]交付
upon [əˈpɒn]		prep. 根据;接近;在……之上
renewal [rɪˈnjuːəl]		n. 更新;恢复
standard [ˈstændə(r)d]		n. 标准;水准
		adj. 标准的;合规格的
union [ˈjuːnjən]		n. 联盟

Exercises

Ⅰ. True or false

a) Often, the road is not wide enough to permit opposing streams of traffic past the work area. Then it is necessary to use "Stop/Slow", where each stream is allowed past the work area in turn.

b) Personal safety is emphasized in all Canada training. This ranges from proper clothing to learning appropriate behavior.

c) The Advanced Worksite Traffic Management (AWTM) requires only one year experience as a qualified TC as a minimum prerequisite, and need also be renewed after two years.

d) Traffic Control Person (TCP) Certification Training has an expiry date of 3 years, upon which the course must be completed again for renewal.

e) While construction traffic control in the U.S. used to be a widely unionized profession, it is now dominated by private business and wages are not controlled by the union.

Ⅱ. Filling blanks

a) If lanes have been closed, large flashing arrows (arrow-boards) on trailers may be to

_____ give motorists hundreds of meters warning to move over. Motorists will be advised they are leaving a worksite by speed reinstatement or "End Roadworks" signs.

b) Sometimes on dual carriageways, it is _____ to divert one carriageway onto the opposing carriageway, forming a "contraflow".

c) The amount of signage required can be _____, needing some hours to put in place. Normally a single two-person crew with one tool is sufficient for most jobs.

d) Accreditation course standards and variations to the Australian Standards are _____ by Main Roads Western Australia (MRWA), part of the Ministry of Planning and Infrastructure.

e) Although the Federal Highway Administration specifies standards and guidelines through the MUTCD which apply to the usage of traffic control equipment, individual state and local agencies can _____ variations or additions to these standards.

III. Translation

a) Traffic control is an outdoors occupation, night or day for long hours in all weathers, and is considered a dangerous occupation due to the high risk of being struck by passing vehicles.

b) A traffic control crew may consist of one person running a simple diversion or closure of a cul-de-sac, up to multiple two- or three-person crews for a complex task.

c) In Nova Scotia training is regulated by the Nova Scotia Department of Transportation and Infrastructure Renewal. There is a one-day course for TCPS and a two-day course for Temporary Workplace Signers.

2.3 Electronic Toll Collection

Electronic toll collection (ETC) aims to eliminate the delay on toll roads by collecting tolls electronically. ETC determines whether the cars passing are enrolled in the program, alerts enforcers for those that are not, and electronically debits the accounts of registered car owners without requiring them to stop.

In 1959, Nobel Economics Prize winner William Vickrey was the first to propose a system of electronic tolling for the Washington Metropolitan Area. He proposed that each car would be equipped with a transponder. "The transponder's personalized signal would be picked up when the car passed through an intersection, and then relayed to a central computer which would calculate the charge according to the intersection and the time of day and add it to the car's bill" Electronic toll collection has facilitated the concession to the private sector of the construction and operation of urban freeways, as well as made feasible the improvement and the practical implementation of road congestion pricing schemes in a limited number of urban areas to restrict auto travel in the most congested areas.

In the 1960s and 1970s, free flow tolling was tested with fixed transponders at the undersides of the vehicles and readers, which were located under the surface of the highway.

Norway has been the world's pioneer in the widespread implementation of this technology. ETC was first introduced in Bergen, in 1986, operating together with traditional tollbooths. In 1991, Trondheim introduced the world's first use of completely unaided full-speed electronic tolling. Norway now has 25 toll roads operating with electronic fee collection (EFC), as the Norwegian technology is called AutoPass. In 1995, Portugal became the first country to apply a single, universal system to all tolls in the country, the Via Verde, which can also be used in parking lots and gas stations. The United States is another country with widespread use of ETC in several states, though many U. S. toll roads maintain the option of manual collection.

Open road tolling (ORT) is a type of electronic toll collection without the use of toll booths. The major advantage to ORT is that users are able to drive through the toll plaza at highway speeds without having to slow down to pay the toll.

2.3.1 Overview

In some urban settings, automated gates are in use in electronic-toll lanes, with 5 mph (8 km/h) legal limits on speed (and 2 to 3 times that as practical limits even with practice and extreme concentration); in other settings, 20 mph (35 km/h) legal limits are not uncommon. However, in other areas such as the Garden State Parkway in New Jersey, and at various locations in California, Florida, Pennsylvania, Delaware, and Texas, cars can travel through electronic lanes at full speed. Illinois' Open Road Tolling program features 274 contiguous miles of barrier-free roadways, where I-PASS or E-ZPass users continue to travel at highway speeds through toll plazas, while cash payers pull off the main roadway to pay at tollbooths. Currently over 80% of Illinois' 1.4 million daily drivers use an I-PASS.

Enforcement is accomplished by a combination of a camera which takes a picture of the car and a radio frequency keyed computer which searches for a driver window/bumper mounted transponder to verify and collect payment. The system sends a notice and fine to cars that pass through without having an active account or paying a toll.

Factors hindering full-speed electronic collection include significant non-participation, entailing lines in manual lanes and disorderly traffic patterns as the electronic- and manual- collection cars "sort themselves out" into their respective lanes; problems with pursuing toll evaders; need, in at least some current (barrier) systems, to confine vehicles in lanes, while interacting with the collection devices, and the dangers of high-speed collisions with the confinement structures; vehicle hazards to toll employees present in some electronic-collection areas; the fact that in some areas at some times, long lines form even to pass through the electronic-collection lanes; and costs and other issues raised when retrofitting existing toll collection facilities. Unionized toll collectors can also be problematic.

Even if line lengths are the same in electronic lanes as in manual ones, electronic tolls save registered cars time: eliminating the stop at a window or toll machine, between successive cars passing the collection machine, means a fixed-length stretch of their journey past it is traveled at a higher average speed, and in a lower time. This is at least a psychological improvement, even if the length of the lines in automated lanes is sufficient to make the no-stop-to-pay savings insignificant compared to time still lost due waiting in line to pass the toll gate. Toll plazas are typically wider than the rest of the highway; reducing the need for them makes it possible to fit toll roads into tight corridors.

Despite these limitations, however, it is important to recognize that throughput increases if delay at the toll gate is reduced (i.e., if the tollbooth can serve more vehicles per hour). The greater the throughput of any toll lane, the fewer lanes required, so expensive construction can be deferred. Specifically, the toll-collecting authorities have incentives to resist pressure to limit the fraction of electronic lanes in order to limit the length of manual-lane lines. In the short term, the greater, the fraction of automated lanes, the lower the cost of operation. In the long term, the greater the relative advantage that registering and turning one's vehicle into an electronic-toll one provides, the faster cars will be converted from manual-toll use to electronic-toll use, and therefore the fewer manual-toll cars will drag down average speed and thus capacity.

Figure 2.13 E-TAG lane on the Second Severn Crossing, Wales

In some countries, some toll agencies (Figure 2.13) that use similar technology have set up (or are setting up) reciprocity arrangements, which permit one to drive a vehicle on another operator's tolled road with the tolls incurred charged to the driver's toll-payment account with their home operator. An example is the United States E-ZPass tag, which is accepted on toll roads, bridges and tunnels in fourteen states from Illinois to Maine.

In Australia, there are a number or organizations that provide tags that can be used on toll roads. They include Roads and Maritime Services, Roam and E-Toll. A toll is debited to the customer's account with their tag provider. Some toll road operators-including Sydney's Sydney Harbor Tunnel, Lane Cove Tunnel, and Westlink M7, Melbourne's Citylink and Eastlink, and Brisbane's Gateway Motorway-encourage use of such tags, and apply an additional vehicle matching fee to vehicles without a tag.

A similar device in France, called Liber-T for light vehicles and TIS-PL for HGVS is accepted on all toll roads in the country.

In Brazil, the Sem Parar/Via-Fácil system allows customers to pass through tolls in more than 1,000 lanes in the states of São Paulo, Paraná, Rio Grande do Sul, Santa Catarina, Bahia and Rio de Janeiro. Sem Parar/Via-Fácil also allows users to enter and exit more than 100 parking lots. There are also other systems, such as via express a onda livre and auto expresso, that are present in the states of Rio de Janeiro, Rio Grande do Sul, Santa Catarina, Parana and Minas Gerais.

In Pakistan, the National Database and Registration Authority is implementing an electronic toll collection system on motorways using RFID.

The European Union has created the EFC-directive, which attempts to standardize European toll collection systems. Systems deployed after 1 January 2007 must support at least one of the following technologies: satellite positioning, mobile communications using the GSM-GPRS standard or 5.8 GHz microwave technology. All toll roads in Ireland must support the eTolltag standard.

2.3.2 Use in Urban Areas and for Congestion Pricing

The most revolutionary application of ETC (Figure 2.14 & Figure 2.15) is in the urban context of congested cities, allowing to charge tolls without vehicles having to slow down. This application made feasible to concession to the private sector the construction and operation of urban freeways, as well as the introduction or improvement of congestion pricing, as a policy to restrict auto travel in downtown areas.

Figure 2.14 ETC at "Costanera Norte" Freeway, crossing downtown 100% free flow, Santiago, Chile

Figure 2.15 Electronic Road Pricing Gantry at North Bridge Road, Singapore

Between 2004 and 2005, Santiago, Chile implemented the world's first 100% full speed electronic tolling with transponders crossing through the city's core (CBD) in a system of several concessioner urban freeways (Autopista Central and Autopista Costanera Norte). The United Arab Emirates implemented in 2007 a similar road toll collection in Dubai, called Salik. Similar schemes were previously implemented but only on bypass or outer ring urban freeways in several cities around the world: Toronto in 1997 (Highway 407), several roads in Norway (AutoPASS), Melbourne in 2000 (CityLink), and Tel Aviv also in 2000.

Congestion pricing or urban toll schemes were implemented to enter the downtown area using ETC technology and/or cameras and video recognition technology to get the plate numbers in several cities around the world: urban tolling in Norway's three major cities: Bergen (1986), Oslo (1990), and Trondheim (1991); Singapore in 1998, as an upgrade to the world's first successful congestion pricing scheme implemented with manual control in 1975; Rome in 2001 as an upgrade to the manual zone control system implemented in 1998; London in 2003 and extended in 2007; Stockholm, tested in 2006 and made the charge permanent in 2007; and in Valletta, the capital city of Malta, since May 2007.

In January 2008, Milan began a one-year trial program called Ecopass, a pollution pricing program in which low-emission-standard vehicles pay a user fee; alternative fuel vehicles and vehicles using conventional fuels but compliant with the Euro IV emission standard are exempted. The program was extended through December 2011 and in January 2012 was replaced by a congestion pricing scheme called Area C.

New York City considered the implementation of a congestion pricing scheme. The proposal was approved by the New York City Council on March 31, 2008, however, on April 7, 2008 the New York State Assembly decided not to vote on the proposal, which means that the plan is stalled.

In 2006, San Francisco transport authorities began a comprehensive study to evaluate the feasibility of introducing congestion pricing. The charge would be combined with other traffic reduction implementations, allowing money to be raised for public transit improvements and bike and pedestrian enhancements. The various pricing scenarios considered were presented in public meetings in December 2008, with final study results expected in 2009.

2.3.3 Technologies

Electronic toll collection systems rely on four major components: automated vehicle identification, automated vehicle classification, transaction processing, and violation enforcement.

The four components are somewhat independent, and, in fact, some toll agencies have contracted out functions separately. In some cases, this division of functions has resulted in difficulties. In one notable example, the New Jersey E-ZPass regional consortium's Violation Enforcement contractor did not have access to the Transaction Processing contractor's database of customers. This, together with installation problems in the automated vehicle identification system, led to many customers receiving erroneous violation notices, and a violation system whose net income, after expenses, was negative, as well as customer dissatisfaction.

1) Automated Vehicle Identification

Figure 2.16 Some highways, such as Ontario's Highway 407 use automatic number plate recognition

Automated vehicle identification (AVI) (Figure 2.16) is the process of determining the identity of a vehicle subject to tolls. The majority of toll facilities record the passage of vehicles through a limited number of toll gates. At such facilities, the task is then to identify the vehicle in the gate area.

Some early AVI systems used barcodes affixed to each vehicle, to be read optically at the toll booth. Optical systems proved to have poor reading reliability, especially when faced with inclement weather and dirty vehicles.

Most current AVI systems rely on radio-frequency identification, where an antenna at the toll gate communicates with a transponder on the vehicle via Dedicated Short Range Communications (DSRC). RFID tags have proved to have excellent accuracy, and can be read at highway speeds. The major disadvantage is the cost of equipping each vehicle with a transponder, which can be a major start-up expense, if paid by the toll agency, or a strong customer deterrent, if paid by the customer.

To avoid the need for transponders, some systems, notably the 407 ETR (Electronic Toll Route) near Toronto, use automatic number plate recognition. Here, a system of cameras captures images of vehicles passing through tolled areas, and the image of the number plate is extracted and used to identify the vehicle. This allows customers to use the facility without any advance interaction with the toll agency. The disadvantage is that fully automatic recognition has a significant error rate, leading to billing errors and the cost of transaction processing (which requires locating and corresponding with the customer) can be significant. Systems that incorporate a manual review stage have much lower error rates, but require a continuing staffing expense.

A few toll facilities cover a very wide area, making fixed toll gates impractical. The most notable of these is a truck tolling system in Germany. This system instead uses Global Positioning System location information to identify when a vehicle is located on a tolled Autobahn. Implementation of this system turned out to be far lengthier and more costly than expected.

As smart phone use becomes more commonplace, some toll road management companies have turned to mobile phone apps to inexpensively automate and expedite paying tolls from the lanes. One such example application is Alabama Freedom Pass mobile, used to link customer accounts at sites operated by American Roads LLC. The app communicates in real time with the facility transaction processing system to identify and debit customer accounts or bill a major credit card.

2) Automated Vehicle Classification

Automated vehicle classification is closely related to automated vehicle identification (AVI). Most toll facilities charge different rates for different types of vehicles, making it necessary to distinguish the vehicles passing through the toll facility.

The simplest method is to store the vehicle class in the customer record, and use the AVI data to look up the vehicle class. This is low-cost, but limits user flexibility, in such cases as the automobile owner who occasionally tows a trailer.

More complex systems use a variety of sensors. Inductive sensors embedded in the road surface can determine the gaps between vehicles, to provide basic information on the presence of a vehicle. Treadles permit counting the number of axles as a vehicle passes over them and, with offset-treadle installations, also detect dual-tire vehicles. Light-curtain laser profilers record the shape of the vehicle, which can help distinguish trucks and trailers.

3) Transaction Processing

Transaction processing deals with maintaining customer accounts, posting toll transactions and customer payments to the accounts, and handling customer inquiries. The transaction processing component of some systems is referred to as a "customer service center". In many respects, the transaction processing function resembles banking, and several toll agencies have contracted out transaction processing to a bank.

Customer accounts may be postpaid, where toll transactions are periodically billed to the customer, or prepaid, where the customer funds a balance in the account which is then depleted as toll transactions occur. The prepaid system is more common, as the small amounts of most tolls makes pursuit of uncollected debts uneconomic. Most postpaid accounts deal with this issue by requiring a security deposit, effectively rendering the account a prepaid one.

4) Violation Enforcement

A violation enforcement system (VES) is useful in reducing unpaid tolls, as an unmanned toll gate otherwise represents a tempting target for toll evasion. Several methods can be used to deter toll violators.

Police patrols at toll gates can be highly effective. In addition, in most jurisdictions, the legal framework is already in place for punishing toll evasion as a traffic infraction. However, the expense of police patrols makes their use on a continuous basis impractical, such that the probability of being stopped is likely to be low enough as to be an insufficient deterrent.

A physical barrier, such as a gate arm, ensures that all vehicles passing through the toll booth have paid a toll. Violators are identified immediately, as the barrier will not permit the violator to proceed. However, barriers also force authorized customers, which are the vast majority of vehicles passing through, to slow to a near-stop at the toll gate, negating much of the speed and capacity benefits of electronic tolling.

Automatic number plate recognition, while rarely used as the primary vehicle identification method, is more commonly used in violation enforcement. In the VES context, the number of images collected is much smaller than in the AVI context. This makes manual review, with its greater accuracy over fully automated methods, practical. However, many jurisdictions require legislative action to permit this type of enforcement, as the number plate identifies only the vehicle, not its operator, and many traffic enforcement regulations require identifying the operator in order to issue an infraction.

An example of this is the toll system on the Illinois Tollway, which requires transponder users to enter their license plate information before using the system. If the transponder fails to read, the license plate number is matched to the transponder account, and the regular toll amount is deducted from the account rather than a violation being generated. If the license plate can't be found in the database, then it is processed as a violation. An interesting aspect of Illinois' toll violation system is a 7 day grace period, allowing tollway users to pay missed tolls online with no penalty the 7 days following the missed toll.

2.3.4 Privacy Issues

Electronic toll collection can be a threat to location privacy. Many implementations are implemented in a privacy-insensitive manner. Using E-Cash and other modern cryptographic methods, it is possible to design systems that do not know where individuals are, but are still able to enforce fares.

New Words and Expressions

collection [kə'lekʃ(ə)n]   n. 采集;聚集;收藏品;
propose [prə'pəʊz]   v. 建议;打算;求婚
transponder [træn'spɒndə(r)]   n. 转调器;变换器;发射器
facilitated [fə'sɪləteɪt]   v. 促进;帮助
construction [kən'strʌkʃ(ə)n]   n. 建设;建筑物
toll [təʊl]   n. 通行费;代价
                  v. 征收;敲钟
currently ['kʌrəntlɪ]   adv. 当前;一般地
payment ['peɪmənt]   n. 付款;支付
evader [ɪ'veɪdə(r)]   n. 逃避者
structure ['strʌktʃə(r)]   n. 结构;构造;建筑物
                  v. 建造
problematic [ˌprɒblə'mætɪk]   adj. 问题的;不确定的
fit [fɪt]   adj. 健康的;恰当的

	n. 合身;发作
delay [dɪˈleɪ]	*n.* 延期;耽搁
defer [dɪˈfɜː(r)]	*v.* 推迟;延期;服从
permanent [ˈpɜː(r)mənənt]	*adj.* 永久的;永恒的;不变的
scheme [skiːm]	*n.* 计划;组合
	v. 计划;策划
proposal [prəˈpəʊz(ə)l]	*n.* 提议;建议
enforcement [ɪnˈfɔː(r)smənt]	*n.* 执行;实施;强制
division [dɪˈvɪʒ(ə)n]	*n.* [数]除法;部门
agency [ˈeɪdʒ(ə)nsɪ]	*n.* 代理;中介
rate [reɪt]	*n.* 比率;率;速度;价格;等级
	v. 认为;估价
credit [ˈkredɪt]	*n.* 信用;信誉
method [ˈmeθəd]	*n.* 方法;条理
deposit [dɪˈpɒzɪt]	*n.* 存款;保证金
	v. 使沉积;存放
deter [dɪˈtɜː(r)]	*v.* 制止;阻止
negate [nɪˈgeɪt]	*v.* 否定;使无效;抹杀;使作废
issue [ˈɪsjuː]	*n.* 问题;流出;期号;
	v. 发行;发布;
design [dɪˈzaɪn]	*v.* 设计;计划;构思
	n. 设计;图案

Exercises

I. True or false

a) Enforcement is accomplished by a combination of a camera which takes a picture of the car and a radio frequency keyed computer which searches for a drivers window/bumper mounted transponder to verify and collect payment.

b) Even if line lengths are the same in electronic lanes as in manual ones, electronic tolls save registered cars time: increasing the stop at a window or toll machine, between successive cars passing the collection machine, means a fixed-length stretch of their journey past it is traveled at a higher average speed, and in a lower time.

c) In Brazil, there are a number or organizations that provide tags that can be used on toll roads.

d) In 2006, San Francisco transport authorities began a comprehensive study to evaluate the feasibility of introducing congestion pricing.

e) Automatic number plate recognition, while rarely used as the primary vehicle identification method, is more commonly used in violation enforcement.

II. Filling blanks

a) The major advantage to ORT is that users are able to drive through the toll plaza at highway speeds _____ having to slow down to pay the toll.

b) The European Union has _____ the EFC-directive, which attempts to standardize European toll collection systems.

c) The program was extended _____ December 2011 and in January 2012 was replaced by a congestion pricing scheme called Area C.

d) Most toll facilities charge different rates for different types of vehicles, making it necessary to _____ the vehicles passing through the toll facility.

e) An example of this is the Toll system on the Illinois Tollway, which requires transponder users to enter their license plate information _____ using the system.

III. Translation

a) Open road tolling (ORT) is a type of electronic toll collection without the use of toll booths. The major advantage to ORT is that users are able to drive through the toll plaza at highway speeds without having to slow down to pay the toll.

b) Enforcement is accomplished by a combination of a camera which takes a picture of the car and a radio frequency keyed computer which searches for a driver window/bumper mounted transponder to verify and collect payment.

c) Electronic toll collection systems rely on four major components: automated vehicle identification, automated vehicle classification, transaction processing, and violation enforcement.

Chapter 3 Advanced Traveler Information Systems (ATIS)

3.1 Overview of ATIS

Adapted from "Development of GIS-based advanced traveler information system (ATIS) in Hong Kong" by S. C. Wong, Master Thesis, 2002

3.1.1 Mechanism of ATIS

With the fast development of economy and the increasing need for social transportation, the restrict effect of transportation to economy development happens universally in each nation with different extent. How to solve traffic congestion and jam phenomena almost becomes a hard nut to crack in each nation.

Advanced Traveler Information System (ATIS) is an integral component of the concept of Intelligent Transportation Systems (ITS). The main function of ATIS is about providing different categories of travelers, mainly road drivers and the public transport users with the right information at the right time and location. The primary services of ATIS are designed to assist travelers in making sound choices by providing pre-trip and en-route travel information concerning traffic conditions and route guidance to improve the quality and convenience of their trips. The travel information is derived based on the data the authority collected on-site or retrieved from the static data inventory. Then the right information is disseminated to the travelers through with the applications of advanced telemetric technologies in different user-specific ATIS services.

ATIS involves the process of on-site and static data acquisition, analysis, communication, information presentation and use of information to assist the travelers to make more informed decision on the route, mode, departure time and any other related to traveling. Figure 3.1 illustrates the whole picture of the information flow in ATIS.

From the very beginning, ATIS developed in line with the emergence of computer technologies and traffic surveillance and control systems. Travel information was disseminated in one-way communication system from information providers, such as Transport Department, to the commuters. It depended on the commuters' decisions to receive what information and how to interpret the information.

Advances in communication, mapping and multimedia technologies motivate the development of more user-specific traveler Information and Location Based Services (LBS) on interactive user interface. With the application of web technologies, wireless telecommunications and internet, mobile computing (handheld/in-vehicle computer) Cable Television, information kiosks, Automatic Vehicle Location (AVL/VLS), In-Vehicle Route Guidance, GPS, GIS and Consumer Electronics (CE), the applications of ATIS achieve a higher level.

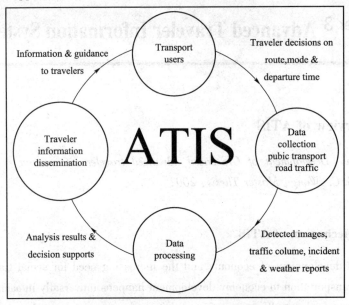

Figure 3.1 Simplified diagram of ATIS operation and information processing

Nowadays with the rapid development of the technologies of High-bandwidth Wireless Network, Third Generation Wireless Communication (3G) Technology, Integrated Services Digital Network (ISDN) and Virtual Reality, traveler information in a large amount of textual and image data could be efficiently disseminated to handheld terminals like smart mobile phones to allow the travelers to comprehend the traffic condition in a timely manner.

3.1.2 Technologies of ATIS

Traffic delays are inevitable given that traffic levels are increasing at a rate faster than new roadways are being built. Advanced travelers information systems (ATIS) and advanced traffic management systems (ATMS) have been proposed and implemented in several metropolitan areas to help mitigate congestion. The two types of systems are often integrated because the successful operation of both requires a sensor network that collects real-time traffic data and an online data analysis package that identify the current or predicts the future states of the system. However, they differ in how the system state information is used. ATIS communicates the information, such as travel time between an origin-destination (O-D) pair on alternative routes, to individual users through various means in an attempt to help them make better travel-related decisions. ATMS in general takes advantage of the information by operating traffic control devices such as traffic lights, ramp meters, and incident management. ATMS sometimes also refers to advanced transportation management systems or automated transportation management systems. In those cases, it usually encompasses both ATIS and ATMS in the narrower sense.

Amongst the technologies, GIS forms an integral part of ATIS. It is one of the advanced computer applications involving the storage and manipulation of the electronic maps and related geographic data with location references. Compared with the traditional storage of travel information on the textual or paper-based maps, GIS provides a powerful tool to visualize the traveler information such as the quickest route to the destination, traffic incident locations, traffic speed presentation on a user-friendly graphical user interface (GUI). It quickens the retrieval, inputting and consolidating process of the traveler information.

An important development within ITS is the emergence and installation of different kinds of sensor technologies for collecting data on the state of the transport system. An important example is the use of GPS for traffic data collection. GPS data and other opportunistic sensors (e. g. smart phones) have great potential to provide the large amounts of data. Intelligent Transportation Systems can make use of these data sources and data from other related sources (e. g. weather, video cameras, etc) to enable real time traffic monitoring and management with a broader scope and sustain-ability than usually achieved.

The GPS data is first received by the source operator and converted to tuples with time stamps, GPS device identification, latitude, longitude, heading (i. e. direction), and instantaneous speed attributes. For the GPS data to be useful for measuring traffic conditions on roads, it must be matched with the underlying road network. An important issue with GPS data is its accuracy. There are two kinds of errors of the GPS data: measurement error caused by the limited GPS accuracy, and the sampling error caused by the sampling rate. The measurement error of GPS devices is typically in the order of a few meters. While this may seem small, this causes a problem when the GPS reading is located close to different links, such as at an intersection. The sampling error causes uncertainty in the vehicle's movement. In order to correct the effect of both kinds of errors, the GPS data is always processed in two steps, called geo-matching and geo-tracking.

3.1.3 Significance of ATIS in Different Parts of the World

ATIS have been studied and implemented in the developed countries like the North Americas, the Europe and Japan since 1950s. Most of these countries have long-history research and development experiences in applying IT to solve different transportation problems. A number of famous ATIS-related projects, such as TravInfo in United States, IMMI in UK are reviewed as follows.

With the increasing popularity of the computers and electronic communication technologies, ATIS have been widely implemented over United States ranging from navigation system to the traffic and traveler information management. Governmental transport agencies in US recognized the significance of applying innovative technologies in transportation operation and planning since early 1950. With the support from the central government especially U.S. DOT (U. S. Department of Transportation), different transportation societies or advocate groups were gradually set up in the local levels to encourage ITS development. One of the most influential societies is the Intelligent Transportation Society of America (ITS America) under which a special committee, named Advanced Traveler Information Systems Committee was established. ITS America establishment was specially featured for its intimate public-private partnership and wide spectrum of member organizations from all levels of government, private sector, academia and ITS international community.

Guiding document on deploying Traveler Information System is prepared by U.S. DOT to reassure consistent nationwide development of integrated and multi-modal Traveler Information System. TravInfo is a multi-modal traveler information system covering San Francisco Bay Area. It collects and integrates the available real-time information on all surface transportations. The major problem TravInfo facing is the disconnection between the user needs and traveler information content due to slow decision making processes among the private and public sectors.

In the United Kingdom, Integrated Multi-modal Information (IMMI) is a fully functional ATIS. Transport Direct of United Kingdom (UK) highlights the ultimate goal of developing ATIS is to enable the traveler to seek information on the whole journey itinerary rather than about a specific mode(s). This has widened the concept of ATIS from merely more accessible information provision to a Travel Itinerary Planner with multi-modal solutions for travelers. It not only assists travelers in planning individual trips but also aids them in planning a sequence of daily travel activities. IMMI provides wide-ranging options on mode, route, destinations, and scheduling to arrange the sequence of stops, suggest and select the stop locations, provide route schedule information and suggest travel routes.

New Words and Expressions

with different extent	有不同程度的
traffic congestion	交通拥堵
disseminated [dɪˈsemɪneɪtɪd]	adj. 弥散性的
in line with	本着
traffic surveillance and control systems	交通监视和控制系统
multimedia technologies	多媒体技术
motivate [ˈməʊtɪveɪt]	vt. 激发(兴趣或欲望); 给予动机
Location Based Services (LBS)	基于位置的服务
mobile computing	移动计算
information kiosks	信息亭
Integrated Services Digital Network	集成业务数字网
Virtual Reality	虚拟现实
mitigate [ˈmɪtɪgeɪt]	vt. 减轻; 缓和
take advantage of	充分利用
manipulation [məˌnɪpjʊˈleɪʃn]	n. 操纵; 控制; 篡改
electronic maps	电子地图
electronic communication technologies	电子通信技术
innovative [ˈɪnəvətɪv]	adj. 创新的; 革新的
multi-modal	多模态
ultimate [ˈʌltɪmət]	adj. 根本的; 极限的; 最后的; 终极
	n. 终极; 极品; 根本

itinerary [aɪˈtɪnəˌrɛrɪ] 　　　　　　*n.* 旅行计划,行程表;旅程;游记
　　　　　　　　　　　　　　　　　　adj. 旅程的;巡回的;游历的

Exercises

I. True or false

a) The travel information is derived based on the data the authority collected on-site or retrieved from the dynamic data inventory.

b) Travel information was disseminated in two-way communication system from information providers, such as Transport Department, to the commuters.

c) Advanced travelers information systems (ATIS) and advanced traffic management systems (ATMS) have been proposed and implemented in several metropolitan areas to help mitigate congestion.

d) ATIS communicates the information, such as travel time between an origin-destination (O-D) pair on alternative routes, to individual users through various means in an attempt to help them make better travel-related decisions.

e) The major problem TravInfo facing is the connection between the user needs and traveler information content due to slow decision making processes among the private and public sectors.

II. Filling blanks

a) How to solve _____ and jam phenomena almost becomes a hard nut to crack in each nation.

b) The right information is _____ to the travelers through with the applications of advanced telemetric technologies in different user-specific ATIS services.

c) ATIS developed in line with the emergence of computer technologies and _____.

d) ATIS communicates the information, such as travel time between an _____ pair on alternative routes, to individual users through various means in an attempt to help them make better travel-related decisions.

e) Governmental transport agencies in US recognized the significance of applying _____ in transportation operation and planning since early 1950.

III. Translation

a) The main function of ATIS is about providing different categories of travelers, mainly road drivers and the public transport users with the right information at the right time and location.

b) The GPS data is first received by the source operator and converted to tuples with time stamps, GPS device identification, latitude, longitude, heading (i.e. direction), and instantaneous speed attributes.

c) Most of these countries have long-history research and development experiences in applying IT to solve different transportation problems.

3.2 Route Choice with Real-time Information

Adapted from "Modeling Strategic Route Choice and Real-Time Information Impacts in Stochastic and Time-Dependent Networks" by Song Gao, published in IEEE Transactions on Intelligent

Over the next few years, driver behavior should become more informed with the advent and deployment of real-time in-vehicle navigation systems. These will provide drivers the fastest path between a current location and final destination, updated in real-time to consider recurring and non-recurring congestion. In the absence of choice, information is of relatively little use. However, many drivers have the opportunity to select dynamically between alternative routes (as well as modes, schedules and activity locations). Over the long term, such systems may reduce the need to construct additional highway infrastructure, or they may induce additional demand. With advanced traveler information system (ATIS) each traveler individually, and the road network as a whole, could be made more productive. Current travelers would save time by being informed, while dynamic (and stochastic) variations in the utilization of transportation capacity could be smoothed out, thereby resulting in a higher traffic throughput. Previous research suggests that ATIS not only reduces the driver's travel time and vehicle operating costs, but also affects (either positively or negatively) the travel time of other commuters.

Traffic networks are inherently uncertain with random disturbances such as incidents, bad weather, work zone and fluctuating demand, which create significant congestion and unreliability. According to the 2009 Urban Mobility Report of the Texas Transportation Institute, such random disturbances account for more than fifty percent of all delay on the roads and the associated wasted fuel and emission. Meanwhile, with the fast development of sensor and telecommunication technologies, real-time information is increasingly available for travelers to make potentially better decisions in such an uncertain system. There are various mechanisms for providing real-time information differing in the spatial and temporal availability, the quality, and the format of information provided, e.g. variables message signs (VMS), websites, radio, traveler information call centers, in-vehicle communication systems connected to traffic management centers and/or other vehicles. It follows that in formulating traveler information related research problems, information should be an explicit part so that traditional simplified assumptions such as full or no information can be avoided.

Travelers' route choices in astochastic network with real-time information are conceivably different from those in a deterministic network. It is generally believed that flexible route choices that adapt to network conditions will save travel time and enhance travel time reliability. For example, in a network with random incidents, if one simply sticks to his/her habitual route, he/she could be stuck in the incident link for a very long time. However, if adequate information is available about the incident and the traveler makes use of it and takes a detour, he/she can save travel time. The detour also helps reduce the prohibitively high travel time in an incident situation, and thus provides more reliable travel time.

We distinguish between two types of responses to real-time information: reactive and strategic. The literature saw a large body of studies on diversion or compliance under information (e.g., at a VMS), yet the modeled adaptation behavior is basically reactive meaning that the travelers decisions before arriving at a VMS do not consider the fact that the VMS will provide updated traffic conditions in the future. In reality, travelers might decide to acquire information as long as there is a reasonable prospect of reward from it. Therefore the fact that a branch of the network has a VMS installed could make it more attractive even before the traveler arrives at the VMS location. A strategic traveler, in this case, is one that considers the availability of information in all later decision stages, not just the current one. Recent empirical studies with computer-based or driving simulator-based experiments show that travelers can make strategic route choices.

The problem of optimal strategic routing decision making for an individual traveler has been studied by various researchers. A general conclusion is that in a flow-independent stochastic time-dependent (STD) network, an individual user's travel objective function value (e.g., expected time, expected schedule delay, variance) from following optimal strategic routing decisions is no higher than that from following an optimal fixed path.

After understanding how an individual traveler makes strategic routing decisions, another research question arises: what will be the network-level impact if many travelers make strategic routing decisions? The demand-supply interaction in a stochastic dynamic network needs to be captured to answer the question. This interaction in a deterministic network (with possible perception errors from the demand side) is captured by a conventional dynamic traffic assignment (DTA) model.

The development of user equilibrium traffic assignment models depends on the modeling of stochasticity. Early developments addressed stochasticity in static traffic assignment methods. The concept of Stochastic User Equilibrium (SUE) is in a SUE network no user believes he can improve his travel time by unilaterally changing routes. In other words, users have random perception errors of the true travel times. A "large sample" approximation is used such that the proportion of travelers that take a given path equals its probability to be chosen by an individual traveler. The SUE problem with flow dependent link costs is studied, with a proof of convergence. These early works are extended later in two directions of modeling stochasticity. The first direction is to abandon the "large sample" assumption and treat the flows (path or link) as random variables, either in an equilibrium or day-to-day stochastic process context. The other direction is to add more sources of stochasticity by treating the underlying travel times, capacities and/or origin-destination (OD) trips as random.

A dynamic traffic assignment model considers users can make strategic route choices in response to real-time information in a stochastic time-dependent network with correlated link travel times. A routing policy is defined as a decision rule which specifies what node to take next out of the current node based the current time and real-time information, essentially a mapping from network states to decisions on next nodes. A routing policy can manifest itself as different paths depending on the underlying stochastic process that drives a traffic network. A path is purely topological and is a special case of a routing policy where any decision on the next node is not dependent on the current time or real-time information.

A similar concept is called "strategy" in the literature of transit assignment. A strategy consists in a rule that assigns to each decision node a set of outgoing arcs, probably sorted in preference order (the so-called "attractive lines"). A traveler follows the first available arc from the preference set. Early studies assume flow-independent probabilities in accessing attractive lines.

As an extension to the static model, a strategic model for dynamic traffic assignment assumes hard arc capacity constraints and holding of traffic, which is suitable for transit networks, but might not be for a traffic network. The randomness in travel times comes from the fact that if the demand for a given arc exceeds its hard capacity, then a given traveler might not be able to access the arc and has to use another arc. No external random events such as incidents or demand fluctuations are modeled. This could limit the model's ability to assess an advanced traveler information system (ATIS) which usually plays an important role when random events happen.

Strategic assignment studies in a traffic network have been restricted in static networks. These studies assume limited spatial stochastic dependency, and that users learn the realized conditions of outgoing links upon reaching a node.

The routing policy based DTA model is the first research endeavor on assigning strategic travelers onto congested, stochastic, and time-dependent traffic networks, by integrating three major components: optimal routing policy generation, routing policy choice model and routing policy loading model. It contributes to the state of the art through the following novel features of the integrated DTA model:

• Users' choice sets comprise of routing policies rather than paths to model travelers' strategic route choices. The strategic choices are dependent on the time-of-day and information on realized flow-dependent link travel times, with possible spatial and/or temporal limitations. Thus the usual simplified assumptions of no information or full information is avoided. The encapsulation of real-time information in the definition of a routing policy makes the general framework naturally suitable to handle heterogeneous information access situations over users.

• Link-wise and time-wise stochastic dependencies of link travel times (which is prominent in reality) are modeled by treating link travel times as jointly distributed time dependent random variables.

• The equilibrium is in terms of probabilistic distributions of time-dependent link travel times and path flows. In other words, traveler's route choices are stable under the equilibrium in the sense of a stable distribution, rather than stable, fixed values.

New Words and Expressions

productive [prə'dʌktɪv]	adj. 多产的, 生产性的
transportation capacity	运输能力
smoothed out	平滑的;
traffic throughput	交通量;
account for	对……负有责任
stochastic [stə'kæstɪk]	adj. 随机
conceivably [kən'siːvəblɪ]	adv. 令人信服地
route choices	路口选择
stick [stɪk]	v. 陷入, 粘住; 刺
detour ['diːtʊər]	v. 绕路

distinguish [dɪ'stɪŋgwɪʃ]	vt. 区分,辨别,使杰出,使表现突出
	vi. 区别,区分,辨别
strategic [strə'tiːdʒɪk]	adj. 战略
optimal strategic routing decisions	最优策略路由决策
network-level	网络层
approximation [əˌprɒksɪ'meɪʃn]	n. 接近
convergence [kən'vɜːdʒəns]	n. [数] 收敛;会聚,集合
manifest ['mænɪfest]	n. 载货单,货单;旅客名单
endeavor [ɪn'devə]	n. 努力
heterogeneous [ˌhetərəʊ'dʒiːniəs]	adj. 各种各样的,由多种种类组成的

Exercises

I. True or false

a) Traffic networks are inherently certain with random disturbances such as incidents, bad weather, work zone and fluctuating demand, which create significant congestion and unreliability.

b) Travelers' route choices in a stochastic network with real-time information are conceivably different from those in a deterministic network.

c) Astatic traffic assignment model considers users can make strategic route choices in response to real-time information in a stochastic time-dependent network with correlated link travel times.

d) A routing policy can manifest itself as different paths independent to the underlying stochastic process that drives a traffic network.

e) The equilibrium is in terms of probabilistic distributions of time-dependent link travel times and path flows.

II. Filling blanks

a) With advanced traveler information system (ATIS) each traveler individually, and the road network as a whole, could be made more _____.

b) According to the 2009 Urban Mobility Report of the Texas Transportation Institute, such random disturbances _____ more than fifty percent of all delay on the roads and the associated wasted fuel and emission.

c) Travelers' route choices in a _____ network with real-time information are conceivably different from those in a deterministic network.

d) A "large sample" _____ is used such that the proportion of travelers that take a given path equals its probability to be chosen by an individual traveler.

e) The routing policy based DTA model is the first research _____ on assigning strategic travelers onto congested, stochastic, and time-dependent traffic networks, by integrating three major components: optimal routing policy generation, routing policy choice model and routing policy loading model.

III. Translation

a) Over the long term, such systems may reduce the need to construct additional highway infrastructure, or they may induce additional demand.

b) Meanwhile, with the fast development of sensor and telecommunication technologies, real-time information is increasingly available for travelers to make potentially better decisions in such an uncertain system.

c) A routing policy is defined as a decision rule which specifies what node to take next out of the current node based the current time and real-time information, essentially a mapping from network states to decisions on next nodes.

3.3 GIS and GPS in ITS

Adapted from "The application of GIS and GPS in ITS" by X. K. Zhou, M. Chen etc., published in 2007 International Conference on Convergence Information Technology, 21st-23rd, Nov, 2007.

Computer technology, communications technology and modern control technology provide reliable guarantee for the construction of ITS. Not only the concrete actor (driver) of traffic action but also the constitutor, manager and surveillant of whole traffic system; not only before traffic action happens (e. g. the routing choice before departing) but also during the process of traffic action (e. g. vehicle navigation) and even after traffic action (e. g. charge and cast accounts), all need many time and space information supports. GIS/GPS technology is the important environment that provides these supports.

GIS is the high and new technology that can save and process spatial information. It combines geography location with relative attributes and export graphics and text datum to users correctly and veritably. GPS is a navigation, location and timer system based on satellite. Receiver computes planar or three dimensional location according to datum supplied by GPS satellite. The combination of GIS and GPS can display and manage moving objects with real-time, and at the same time provides material query of geography information database and knock-down technology means for the realization of ITS, and is the bridge of real-time and dynamic observation and communications technology that realizes spatial actions. Thereinto, the vehicle navigation with real-time, surveillance and control is the most primary and comprehensive item in the applications of GIS and GPS in ITS.

The vehicle navigation system is composed of GPS navigation, autonomic navigation, embed technology, vehicle's speed sensor, peg-top sensor and LCD display. It combines with GIS, wireless communications technology and computer vehicles management information system, then form a GIS/GPS compositive service network. Consequently we can realize the functions of GIS/GPS in ITS as follows:

1) GIS Graphic Manipulations Function and Real-time Locate Vehicle Function

It can finish the zoom in, zoom out, layered display, move of GIS electronic map, attributes display, fuzzy query, query attributes according map or query map according attributes, measure distance and area, the multilevel display of map, display in different windows functions and so on.

We use the compositive applications of GPS signal, vehicle's speed sensor, peg-top sensor to generate the information of vehicle's real-time location, and display on the display according to GIS electronic map. The map can be zoomed by user's wanted ratio and can scan with the vehicle's location.

2) Optimize Routing

Using GIS platform, users may set, plan, save and modify the optimum path of trip according to the starting and finishing point of trip and guide driver to run by the optimum path, so the efficiency of traveling can be enhanced.

Firstly, the basic rule is the static optimal path planning. Its weight of pathway is mainly the length of the road, the information of history traffic or other information. We can use table of two dimension relationship store the weight of pathway. It's very convenience to extract data and can enhance computing efficiency.

Secondly, the extended rule is dynamic optimal path planning. Its characteristic is that system can receive and process real-time information of dynamic road traffic, and the information can be storage into database by time order. When the path is planned, the dynamic information of traffic are assigned to the network by some way, which is seen as weight of pathway when we plan the optimal path, and then based on the weight of pathway we compute optimal path planning that meets traveler's certain need. Then the optimal path meeting passenger's one rule can be work out, based on the weight of pathway. After a certain time, the system will be re-plan the optimal path, the information of traffic used is always new, to ensure that the result is reliable at the planning time.

3) Real-time Navigation

We can locate the current location of vehicle with real-time and veracity according to receiving GPS signal. We use the optimal routing obtained by optimal routing algorithm to guide vehicle to run. During navigation in order not to disrupt the attention of driver, we use the method of phonic cue to guide vehicles. Navigation is classified into the follow two kinds:

(1) Independent Navigation Location

It is independent for the vehicle. The moving vehicle mensurate its location in the geography space itself and realize the functions of object search, routing guide and information query by means of GIS electronic map.

(2) Tracker, Surveillance and Control Navigation Location

This kind of location is the combination of GPS system and vehicle's communications system. We can use vehicle's communications system to send GPS signal to the control center and the center track, supervise and control the vehicle.

4) Intelligent Scheduling

The traffic management center manoeuvres and tracks vehicles according to the real-time location of vehicles. Thereby we can know the real situation of vehicles fully and manoeuvre vehicles in time, which can enhance the efficiency of the vehicles, improve the corresponsive ability to accidents and ameliorate the management of vehicles and the traffic status.

5) Inspection of Traffic Flowage and Accident Analysis

In order to analyze different aspects of traffic, we use the real-time road datum obtained by

GPS and integrate other traffic datum to provide the real-time flowage of road, and also provide the traffic situation of many roads.

What's more, we can use the GPS information saved in system redisplay the accidents that have already happened. Managers can obtain the causes of accidents according to the situation of that day. It can improve the speed of affirming and processing accidents and find out the road that accidents happen frequently, which is very important to the future defence.

6) The Real-time Acquisition Tagging of Transport Facilities Information

Transport facilities information is an important element of intelligent traffic management datum. As transportation details, such as traffic lights control information, pedestrian street, a one-way street and no left turning. The situation of highway, the number of lanes, speed limits and other transport related information in real world change frequently. It's very important for traffic management and road trip planning to master the locations and change of transport facilities. We can use GPS to collect information correctly and complement in time.

7) Other Functions

Besides, there are many other functions. Information service provides the information of road and weather and so on; urgent succor can inform the traffic center to get help by navigation system when the vehicle meets urgent situation; the moving vehicle security management can record insecure actions on the road, which is very convenient to process and correct in time and so on.

The combination of GPS, GIS and communications technology makes people understand the applications of spatial information deeply. In order to make the functions of GPS/GIS in ITS exert effectively, it's better to solve the data fusion, transmission and relative technologies, including location precision, map matching precision, the data fusion on the control platform and distributed database technologies, which can realize the effective integration of relative technologies. With the development of network and other computer science technologies, which can improve the functions of GIS/GPS continuously, the development of ITS in China can be promoted greatly.

New Words and Expressions

modern control technology	现代控制技术
surveillant [sɜːˈveɪlənt]	n. 监视者;监督者
	adj. 监视的;监督的
text datum	文本数据;文本资料
three dimensional location	三维空间
knock-down technology	可拆卸的技术
thereinto [ˌðeərˈɪntuː]	adv. 在其中,在那里面
vehicle navigation system	汽车导航系统
combine with	与……结合
wireless communications technology	无线通信技术
compositive [kəmˈpɒzɪtɪv]	adj. 合成的,综合的
electronic map	电子地图
optimum [ˈɒptɪməm]	n. 优化

veracity ['vəˈræsətɪ]   n. 诚实;精确性;说真实话
phonic cue ['fɔnɪk]   语音的提示
mensurate ['mensjuəreɪt]   vt. 测定;测量
ameliorate [əˈmiːlɪəreɪt]   vt. 改善;减轻(痛苦等)
    vi. 变得更好
succor ['sʌkə]   n. 救援;援助者
    vt. 救援;援助
precision [prɪˈsɪʒn]   n. 精度,[数] 精密度;精确
    adj. 精密的,精确的
integration [ˌɪntɪˈgreɪʃən]   n. 集成;综合

Exercises

I. True or false

a) GPS combines geography location with relative attributes and export graphics and text datum to users correctly and veritably.

b) The combination of GIS and GPS can display and manage moving objects with real-time, and at the same time provides material query of geography information database and knock-down technology means for the realization of ITS, and is the bridge of real-time and dynamic observation and communications technology that realizes spatial actions.

c) The vehicle navigation system is composed of GIS, autonomic navigation, embed technology, vehicle's speed sensor, peg-top sensor and LCD display.

d) Using GIS platform, users may set, plan, save and modify the optimum path of trip according to the starting and finishing point of trip and guide driver to run by the optimum path, so the efficiency of traveling can be enhanced.

e) When the path is planned, the dynamic information of traffic are assigned to the network by some way, which is seen as weight of pathway when we plan the optimal path, and then based on the weight of pathway we compute optimal path planning that meets traveler's certain need.

II. Filling blanks

a) It _____ GIS, wireless communications technology and computer vehicles management information system, then form a GIS/GPS compositive service network.

b) We can use table of two _____ relationship store the weight of pathway.

c) We can locate the current location of vehicle with real-time and _____ according to receiving GPS signal.

d) Thereby we can know the real situation of vehicles fully and manoeuvre vehicles in time, which can enhance the efficiency of the vehicles, improve the corresponsive ability to accidents and _____ the management of vehicles and the traffic status.

e) Transport _____ information is an important element of intelligent traffic management datum.

III. Translation

a) GPS is a navigation, location and timer system based on satellite.

b) We use the compositive applications of GPS signal, vehicle's speed sensor, peg-top sensor to generate the information of vehicle's real-time location, and display on the display according to GIS electronic map.

c) The situation of highway, the number of lanes, speed limits and other transport related information in real world change frequently.

Chapter 4 Advanced Vehicle Control Systems(AVCS)

4.1 Intelligent Vehicle Technology

Adapted from "Intelligent vehicle technology and trends" by Richard Bishop, published in Artech Hous Publishers, May 2005.

4.1.1 Definition of Intelligent Vehicle Technology

Because the term "Intelligent Vehicles" is somewhat generic, a definition is in order for the purposes of this book. Simply put, intelligent vehicle systems sense the driving environment and provide information or vehicle control to assist the driver in optimal vehicle operation. Intelligent vehicle systems operate at the tactical level of driving (throttle, brakes, steering) as contrasted with strategic decisions such as route choice, which might be supported by an on-board navigation system.

Intelligent vehicle systems are seen as a next generation beyond current active safety systems, which provide relatively basic control assist but do not sense the environment or assess risk. Antilock braking systems, traction control, and electronic stability control are examples of such systems.

4.1.2 Application Areas of Intelligent Vehicle Technology

The range of applications for intelligent vehicle systems is quite broad and applies to all types of road vehicles—cars, heavy trucks, and transit buses. While there is some overlap between the functions, and the underlying technology can in some cases support many functions at once, intelligent vehicle applications can generally be classified into four categories: convenience, safety, productivity, and traffic assist.

The following sections describe applications in these areas along with basic information regarding products and supporting technologies to provide context.

Intelligent vehicle applications can be implemented via autonomous or cooperative systems.

Autonomous systems rely upon onboard sensors to provide raw data for a particular application, whereas cooperative systems augment onboard sensor data with information flowing to the vehicle from an outside source. Using wireless communications techniques, this data can be derived from infrastructure sensors or via information sharing with other vehicles. Data from other vehicles can be received either directly through vehicle-vehicle communications or through an innovative technique called floating car data (FCD) or "probe data." The FCD concept relies upon vehicles reporting basic information relevant to traffic, road, and weather conditions to a central data center, which is aggregated and processed to develop a highly accurate picture of conditions across the road network and then disseminated back to vehicles.

In the discussion below, the reader will gain an applications-level understanding of how both autonomous and cooperative techniques can be employed.

4.1.2.1 Convenience Systems

The term "convenience system" came into being in the late nineties when auto companies were ready to offer intelligent vehicle driver-assist systems to their customers but were not yet ready to take on the legal implications and performance requirements that would come with introducing a new product labeled as a "safety system". Fundamentally, convenience systems are driver-support products that may assist the driver in vehicle control to reduce the stress of driving. In some cases these products are safety-relevant—and drivers commonly consider them to be safety systems—but they are not marketed as safety systems.

1) Adaptive Cruise Control (ACC)

The primary convenience system currently available for highway driving is ACC.

ACC allows a driver to set a desired speed as in normal cruise control; if a vehicle immediately ahead of the equipped vehicle is moving at a slower speed, then throttle and braking of the host vehicle is controlled to match the speed of the slower vehicle at a driver-selectable time headway, or gap. The desired speed is automatically reattained when the roadway ahead is unobstructed, either from the slower vehicle ahead leaving the lane or the driver of the host vehicle changing to a clear lane.

These operating modes are illustrated in Figure 4.1. Systems currently on the market monitor the forward scene using either radar or lidar (laser radar); future systems may also use machine vision.

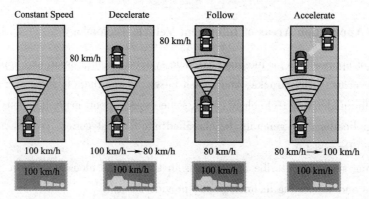

Figure 4.1 Operating modes for ACC

Current generation ACC systems operate only above a speed threshold on the order of 40 km/hr. The braking authority of the system is limited; if the host vehicle is closing very rapidly on a vehicle ahead and additional braking is needed to avoid a crash, the driver is alerted to intervene.

Users generally report that the system substantially reduces the tedium of braking and accelerating in typical highway traffic, in areas where conventional cruise control is all but unusable due to the density of the surrounding traffic.

2) Low-Speed ACC

Low-speed ACC is an evolution of ACC functionality, which operates in slow, congested traffic to follow the car immediately ahead. When traffic clears and speeds return to normal, conventional ACC would then be used. This type of product is sometimes called "stop-and-go ACC". Early versions may only perform a "stop and wait" function, requiring that the driver initiate a resumption of forward movement when appropriate. This is because manufacturers are hesitant to offer a system that automatically starts from a stop in complex low-speed traffic environments, which may include pedestrians. Other low-speed ACC systems operate down to a very low speed (approximately 5 km/h) and then require the driver to intervene if needed to both stop and restart vehicle motion. Low-speed ACC was introduced to the Japanese market in 2004.

3) Lane-Keeping Assistance (LKA)

LKA offers a "copilot" function to drivers in highway environments. Research has shown that the many minute steering adjustments that must be made by drivers on long trips are a significant source of fatigue. LKA uses machine vision technology to detect the lane in which the vehicle is traveling, and steering actuation to add torque to the steering wheel to assist the driver in these minute steering adjustments. The experience can be imagined as similar to driving in a trough, such that the curving vertical sides of the trough create a natural steering resistance to keep the vehicle in the center. As the developers are fond of saying, the experience is "like driving in a bathtub".

Lane-keeping systems generally are set to operate only at the speeds and typical curvatures of major highways, such as the U.S. interstate highway system or major motorways in Europe and Japan. The system will disengage if sharp curves are encountered. Further, the driver must continue to provide steering inputs; otherwise the system will sound an alarm and turn off—this is to ensure that drivers are not tempted to use it as a "hands-off" system.

More advanced versions of LKA could conceivably allow for full automatic "hands-off" steering, but driver vigilance issues would have to first be worked out.

4) "Automated Vehicle Control" & "Parking Assist"

We will discuss them in Section 4.2 and Section 4.3.

4.1.2.2 Safety Systems

Traffic fatalities range into the tens of thousands in developed countries and the numbers of crashes are in the millions. Given the massive societal costs, governments are highly motivated to promote active safety systems for crash avoidance.

Further, based on experience with airbag systems, it has been well established that "safety sells" in the automotive showroom, and therefore automotive manufacturers have a good business case for offering active safety systems on new cars.

Active safety system applications within the intelligent vehicle realm are many and varied.

From the following list of collision countermeasures, it can be seen that virtually every aspect of vehicle crashes is represented:

- Assisting driver perception.

- Adaptive headlights;
- Night vision;
- Animal warning;
- Headway advisory.
• Crash prevention.
- Forward collision warning/mitigation/avoidance;
- Lane departure warning;
- Lane/road departure avoidance;
- Curve speed warning;
- Side object warning (blind spot);
- Lane change support;
- Rollover countermeasures;
- Intersection collision countermeasures;
- Rear impact countermeasures;
- Backup/parking assist;
- Pedestrian detection and warning.
• Degraded driving.
- Driver impairment monitoring;
- Road surface condition monitoring.
• Precrash.
- Prearming airbags;
- Occupant sensing (to inform airbag deployment);
- Seatbelt pretensioning;
- Precharging of brakes.
• External vehicle speed control.

1) Assisting Driver Perception

Intelligent vehicle systems can enhance the driver's perception of the driving environment, leaving any interpretation or action to the driver's judgment. Adaptive headlights provide better illumination when the vehicle is turning; night vision provides an enriched view of the forward scene; roadside systems can alert drivers to the presence of wildlife; and headway advisory provides advice to the driver regarding following distance.

(1) Adaptive Front Lighting (AFS)

Adaptive headlights illuminate areas ahead and to the side of the vehicle path in a manner intended to optimize nighttime visibility for the driver. Basic systems, already on the market, take into account the vehicle speed to make assumptions as to the desired illumination pattern. For instance, beam patterns adjust down and outward for low-speed driving, while light distribution is longer and narrower at high speeds to increase visibility at farther distances. More advanced systems also incorporate steering-angle data and auxiliary headlights on motorized swivels. In the case of a vehicle turning a corner, for example, the outer headlight maintains a straight beam pattern while the inner, auxiliary headlight beam illuminates the upcoming turn. The system aims to automatically deliver a light beam of optimal intensity to maximize the illumination of oncoming road curves and bends. Next generation adaptive lighting systems will use satellite positioning and digital maps so as to have preview information on upcoming curves. Headlights are then aimed into the curve even before the vehicle reaches the curve, at just the right point in the maneuver, to present the driver an optimal view.

(2) Night Vision

Night vision systems help the driver see objects such as pedestrians and animals on the road or the road edge, far beyond the view of the vehicle's headlights. Typically this is displayed via a heads-up display. Advanced forms of night vision process the image to identify potential hazards and highlight them on the displayed image.

(3) Animal Warning

Obviously, not all cars have night vision systems. To provide alerts to wildlife near roads for all drivers, road authorities are experimenting with roadside sensors that detect wildlife such as deer and elk in areas where they are known to be frequently active. If animals are present, drivers are advised by electronic signs as they approach the area.

(4) Headway Advisory

The headway advisory function, also called safe gap advisory, monitors the distance and time headway to a preceding vehicle to provide continuous feedback to the driver. Gap thresholds can be applied to indicate to the driver when safety is compromised. Fundamentally, headway advisory performs the sensing job of ACC without the automatic control.

2) Crash Prevention

The following sections describe crash prevention systems in various stages of development. Some are in the R&D stages, while others have been introduced to the public as optional equipment on new cars.

(1) Forward Collision Warning/Mitigation/Avoidance

Intelligent vehicle safety systems augment the driver's monitoring of the road and traffic conditions to detect imminent crash conditions. Systems to prevent forward collisions rely on radar or lidar sensing, sometimes augmented by machine vision. Basic systems provide a warning to the driver, using a variety of means such as audible alerts, visual alerts (typically on a heads-up display), seat vibration, or even slight seat-belt tensioning to provide a haptic cue. More advanced systems add automatic braking of the vehicle if the driver is not responding to the situation. An initial version of active braking systems is termed "collision mitigation system." These systems primarily defer to the driver's control; braking serves only to reduce the impact velocity of a collision if the driver is not responding appropriately to an imminent crash situation. Collision mitigation systems were originally introduced to the market in Japan in 2003. The next functional level, forward collision avoidance, represents the ultimate crash avoidance system, in which sufficient braking is provided to avoid the crash altogether.

(2) Lane Departure Warning Systems(LDWS)

LDWS use machine vision techniques to monitor the lateral position of the vehicle within its lane. Computer algorithms process the video image to "see" the road markings and gauge the vehicle's position within them. The driver is warned if the vehicle starts to leave the lane inadvertently (i.e., turn signal not activated). A favored driver interface is to emulate the "rumble strip" experience by providing a low rumbling sound on the left or right audio speaker, as appropriate to the direction of the lane departure. LDWS were initially sold in the heavy truck market; they were first introduced to the public in Japan and entered the European and U.S. automobile markets in 2004.

(3) Lane/Road Departure Avoidance (RDA)

Lane departure avoidance systems go one step farther than LDWS by providing active steering to keep the vehicle in the lane (while alerting the driver to the situation). In the case of RDA, advanced systems assess factors such as shoulder width to adjust the driver alert based on the criticality of the situation. For instance, a vehicle drifting onto a wide, smooth road shoulder is a relatively benign event compared to the same situation with no shoulder.

Prototypes of such RDA systems are currently being evaluated.

(4) Curve Speed Warning

Curve speed warning is another form of road departure avoidance that uses digital maps and satellite positioning to assess a safe speed threshold for an upcoming curve in the roadway. The driver is warned if speed is excessive as the vehicle approaches the curve. Prototypes of curve speed warning systems have been built and evaluated.

(5) Side Object Warning

Side object monitoring systems assist drivers in changing lanes by detecting vehicles in the "blind spot" to the left rear of the vehicle (or right rear for countries such as Japan with right side driver positions and left-hand road driving). Blind spot monitoring using radar technology has been used by truckers in the United States for many years and is expected to enter the automobile market soon. Figure 4.2 shows detection zones for side object awareness, as well as other applications. This is a good example of "bundling" such applications.

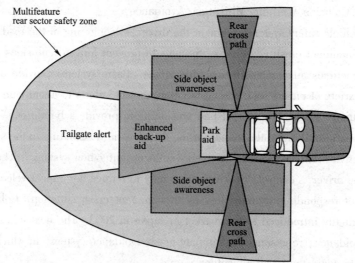

Figure 4.2 Detection zones for side object awareness and other applications

(6) Lane Change Support

Lane change support systems extend monitoring beyond the blind spot to provide rearward sensing to assist drivers in making safe lane changes. Advanced systems also look far upstream in adjacent lanes to detect fast approaching vehicles that may create a hazardous situation in the event of a lane change. This is especially important on high-speed motorways such as the German Autobahn. These systems are in the advanced development phase.

(7) Rollover Countermeasures

Rollover countermeasures systems are designed to prevent rollovers by heavy trucks. While electronic stability control to avoid rollovers of passenger cars is becoming widely available, the vehicle dynamics for tractor trailers are very different—the truck driver is unable to sense the initial trailer "wheels-up" condition that precedes a rollover, and rollover dynamics change with the size and consistency of the cargo. Rollover countermeasure systems approximate the center of gravity of the vehicle and dynamically assess the combination of speed and lateral acceleration to warn the driver when close to a rollover threshold. Systems currently on the market automatically slow the vehicle to avoid the rollover event. Rollover countermeasures systems recently became available in the heavy truck market.

(8) Intersection Collision Countermeasures

Intersection collisions represent a disproportionate amount of the fatal collisions since vehicles often collide at right angles and with significant speed. Development of intersection collision countermeasures systems represents a significant challenge, as threat conditions often cannot be detected by vehicle sensors alone. This is because, at many intersections, crossing traffic may be obscured by buildings near the road or other vehicles. In such cases, cooperative road-vehicle systems are used: Roadside systems detect dangerous situations, such as a vehicle violating a traffic signal, and communicate that information to drivers. Initial systems will warn drivers via roadside signs, and more advanced future systems will also provide the information on in-vehicle displays when communications connectivity is available in vehicles. Another approach to ICA calls for vehicles to communicate their direction and speed to each other as they approach an intersection, with processing and interpretation of that data occurring onboard each vehicle to assess any hazards. In this case, no roadside infrastructure is involved. All such intersection collision countermeasures are currently in the research stage.

(9) Rear Impact Countermeasures

Rear impacts are a particular problem for transit buses that make passenger stops on busy city or suburban streets where other traffic would not normally stop. These buses are susceptible to being struck from behind by following vehicles whose drivers are inattentive. Since the bus is most at risk, rear impact countermeasures rely upon sensing hardware on the rear of the bus to detect fast closing vehicles. When this situation is detected, vivid warning flashers are activated to—it is hoped—attract the following driver's attention in time to avoid a crash.

(10) Backup/Parking Assist

Backup/parking assist systems were described in the convenience systems section, but they can also play a role in avoiding the tragic accidents that occur when small children, who cannot be seen by the driver, are struck by a backing vehicle. Backup assist systems under development use radar or infrared technology to detect children or animals behind the vehicle and highlight this on a video display of the rearward view. Such systems are still several years away from market introduction.

(11) Pedestrian Detection and Warning

Pedestrian detection systems are most useful in urban city centers, where pedestrians are walking near traffic and could decide at any time or place to cross the street. In these situations, sensing systems, typically based on machine vision, must perform real-time processing to detect pedestrians, monitor their movements, and assess the potential danger when pedestrians enter the roadway. Robust detection of pedestrians while avoiding false alarms presents a major challenge to the technical community; nevertheless, steady progress is being made, and first generation systems are in advanced development.

3) Degraded Driving

In degraded driving conditions, the driver is impaired (due to alcohol or fatigue, for example), or the road surface may be degraded, typically due to inclement weather.

(1) Driver Impairment Monitoring

Impaired driver detection has been the subject of extensive scientific study. Basic systems that can detect severe drowsiness have been developed using various methods. Monitoring of lane-tracking behavior, steering inputs by the driver, head movements, and eyelid movements are among the primary methods examined. A key challenge is to detect the early signs of the onset of drowsiness, so that a driver can effectively respond to a warning before drowsiness is severe. These systems can take the form of a "fatigue meter" that provides continuous feedback to the driver, or a warning that sounds when dangerous fatigue conditions are detected. Basic driver drowsiness monitors were on the market in Japan for a short time during the 1980s. First generation products targeted at long-haul truck drivers are currently being sold in the aftermarket, and driver-monitoring products are currently in development for the automobile market.

(2) Road Surface Condition Monitoring

Knowledge regarding degraded road surface conditions, such as wet or icy pavement, is obviously important to the driver. This information can also enable ACC systems to adjust intervehicle gaps and crash countermeasures systems to adjust warning timing based on lower traction, for instance. Spot conditions can be detected to some degree by vehicle systems such as anti-lock braking and traction control, but the ideal case is to have advance knowledge. Such advance warning can be provided by roadside detectors that send messages to the vehicle, or from other vehicles through floating car data techniques or vehicle-vehicle communications.

4) Precrash

The precrash domain refers to the case where sensing systems (typically using ACC sensors) have determined that a crash is inevitable; therefore, action is taken to optimally protect the vehicle occupants via seatbelt pretensioning and prearming or prefiring airbags. In addition, the braking system can be precharged so that maximum braking force is provided immediately upon initiation by the driver.

Precrash systems are generally seen as precursors to more advanced collision avoidance systems, as a bridge between occupant protection measures, which are very mature technologically, and crash avoidance measures, which are in earlier stages of development and product maturity.

5) External Vehicle Speed Control (EVSC)

EVSC, also called intelligent speed adaptation (ISA), assists drivers in keeping the vehicle's speed to the government-defined speed limit.

Proponents of EVSC include residents of small towns through which highways pass. Too often, long-distance drivers do not slow down sufficiently when entering the town, creating safety concerns for residents. Residents of urban neighborhoods have similar concerns when their roads are used as "shortcuts" by commuters to avoid traffic jams on major roadways. More generally, government initiatives to totally eliminate traffic fatalities include a strong component to keep vehicle speeds to the legal limit.

The emerging EVSC approach is to use onboard satellite positioning working in conjunction with a digital map database that includes speed limits for the road network.

Via an active accelerator pedal, the vehicle will automatically "resist" attempts to drive faster than the speed limit; however, the system can be overridden in the case.

4.1.2.3 Productivity Systems

The concept of productivity applies to commercial vehicles and transit buses. Productivity can be increased in terms of operational cost (such as fuel consumption) or time (such as more efficient maneuvering).

4.1.2.4 Traffic-Assist Systems

Congestion has been with us for a very long time, entering the scene not long after the proverbial invention of the wheel. Traffic congestion is a pervasive ill within society, but due to the distributed nature of road traffic, congestion is a "distributed disaster" as distinct from the "spot disasters" of road crashes. Therefore, enhancing safety generally gets higher priority within government programs.

Also, safety improvements are a more tractable domain as compared to addressing traffic congestion—a crash avoidance system on a single vehicle can be highly effective and marketed in new cars, whereas many cars must be equipped and cooperating either with the roadway or each other (or both) for traffic flow to be improved.

At the same time, it must be said that, in industrialized countries, traffic congestion affects the lives of hundreds of millions of drivers every day, whereas safety critical situations—as encountered by individual drivers—are rare by comparison. From both a societal perspective and a market-pull viewpoint, there is ample reason to develop technological means of reducing congestion, if it is indeed possible.

Many government ITS programs focus on managing existing congestion rather than improving traffic flow, with roadway expansion and new roads seen as the only way to combat congestion. The prevailing view is that "there is nothing we can do" to improve traffic and we must learn to "live with it." However, intelligent vehicle systems combining vehicle communications with advanced vehicle control techniques offer the potential for improving traffic flow in the long term. In this respect, the potential of intelligent vehicle systems that improve traffic flow through cooperation between vehicles and the road operator have long been studied in the academic research domain and have recently attracted the attention of automotive laboratories. Several forms of traffic-assist systems have been proposed, simulated, prototyped, and tested: Vehicle Flow Management (VFM), Traffic-Responsive Adaptation, Traffic Jam Dissipation, Start-Up Assist, Cooperative ACC (C-ACC) and Platooning.

New Words and Expressions

antilock braking systems	防抱死系统
traction control	牵引力控制
electronic stability control	电子稳定控制
intelligent vehicle	智能汽车
tactical['tæktɪk(ə)l]	adj. 战术的,策略上的
throttle['θrɔt(ə)l]	n. 油门,节流阀
on-board navigation system	车载导航系统
unobstructed['ʌnəb'strʌktɪd]	adj. 畅通无阻的,不备阻塞
lidar (laser radar)	n. 激光雷达
threshold['θreʃˌhəʊld]	n. 阈值,临界值
Lane-Keeping Assistance(LKA)	车道保持辅助
copilot['kəʊˌpaɪlət]	n. 副驾驶员
fatigue[fə'tiːg]	n. 疲劳
bathtub['bɑːθˌtʌb]	n. 澡盆,浴缸
curvature['kɜː(r)vətʃə(r)]	n. 曲率,曲度,弯曲
interstate highway	州际公路
countermeasure['kaʊntəmeʒə(r)]	n. 对策,反措施
illumination[ɪˌluːmɪ'neɪʃ(ə)n]	n. 照明
perception[pə(r)'sepʃ(ə)n]	n. 感觉,感知,知觉
adaptive headlights	自适应头灯
night vision	夜视系统
animal warning	动物警告
headway advisory	行车间隔报告
crash prevention	事故预防
forward collision warning/mitigation/avoidance	前碰撞警告/缓冲/避免
mitigation[ˌmɪtɪ'geɪʃ(ə)n]	n. 缓解,减轻
imminent['ɪmɪnənt]	adj. 即将发生的,危急的
lane departure warning	车道偏离预警
lateral['læt(ə)rəl]	adj. 侧面的,横向的
lane/road departure avoidance	车道偏离避免
benign[bə'naɪn]	adj. 温和的
curve speed warning	弯道速度预警
side object warning (blind spot)	盲点预警

lane change support	变道支持
adjacent[əˈdʒeɪs(ə)nt]	adj. 邻近的,毗邻的
rollover countermeasures	防翻滚
intersection collision countermeasures	路口碰撞对策
disproportionate[ˌdɪsprəˈpɔː(r)ʃ(ə)nət]	adj. 不成比例的,不相称的
rear impact countermeasures	追尾预防
susceptible[səˈseptəb(ə)l]	adj. 易受影响的,易受感染的
backup/parking assist	停车辅助
pedestrian detection and warning	行人检测及警告
degraded driving	降级行驶
driver impairment monitoring	驾驶人伤情监测
inclement[ɪnˈklemənt]	adj. 恶劣的
drowsiness[ˈdraʊzɪnəs]	n. 睡意,嗜睡
road surface condition monitoring	路况检测
precrash	预撞击
prearming airbags	安全气囊
seatbelt pretensioning	预紧式安全带
external vehicle speed control	外部车速控制
fatality[fəˈtæləti]	n. 死亡(事故),灾祸
proverbial[prəˈvɜː(r)biəl]	adj. 众所周知的,出名的

Exercises

Ⅰ. True or false

a) The primary convenience system currently available for highway driving is ACC.

b) Lane-keeping Assistance system will disengage if gentle curves are encountered.

c) Intelligent vehicle systems can enhance the driver's perception of the driving environment, leaving any interpretation or action to the driver's judgment.

d) In the case of RDA, a vehicle drifting onto a wide, smooth road shoulder is a relatively difficult event compared to the same situation with no shoulder.

e) The emerging EVSC approach is to use onboard satellite positioning working in conjunction with a digital map database that includes speed limits for the road network.

Ⅱ. Filling blanks

a) Intelligent vehicle applications can generally be classified into four categories: _____, safety, productivity, and traffic assist.

b) Adaptive Cruise Control systems currently on the market monitor the forward scene using either _____ or lidar; future systems may also use machine vision.

c) The _____ function, also called safe gap advisory, monitors the distance and time headway to a preceding vehicle to provide continuous feedback to the driver.

d) In _____ conditions, the driver is impaired (due to alcohol or fatigue, for example), or the road surface may be degraded, typically due to inclement weather.

e) External Vehicle Speed Control, also called _____ , assists drivers in keeping the vehicle's speed to the government-defined speed limit.

III. Translation

a) Intelligent vehicle systems are seen as a next generation beyond current active safety systems, which provide relatively basic control assist but do not sense the environment or assess risk. Antilock braking systems, traction control, and electronic stability control are examples of such systems.

b) Fundamentally, convenience systems are driver-support products that may assist the driver in vehicle control to reduce the stress of driving. In some cases these products are safety-relevant—and drivers commonly consider them to be safety systems—but they are not marketed as safety systems.

c) Traffic fatalities range into the tens of thousands in developed countries and the numbers of crashes are in the millions. Given the massive societal costs, governments are highly motivated to promote active safety systems for crash avoidance.

4.2 The Self-Driving Car

4.2.1 Self-driving Cars: on the Cusp of Revolutionary Change

For the past hundred years, innovation within the automotive sector has brought major technological advances, leading to safer, cleaner, and more affordable vehicles. But for the most part, since Henry Ford introduced the moving assembly line, the changes have been incremental, evolutionary. Now, in the early decades of the 21st century, the industry appears to be on the cusp of revolutionary change—with potential to dramatically reshape not just the competitive landscape but also the way we interact with vehicles and, indeed, the future design of our roads and cities. The revolution, when it comes, will be engendered by the advent of autonomous or "self-driving" vehicles. And the timing may be sooner than you think.

The revolution, when it comes, will be engendered by the advent of autonomous or "self-driving" vehicles. And the timing may be sooner than you think.

4.2.2 Google Driverless Car

The Google driverless car is a project by Google that involves developing technology for autonomous cars. The software powering Google's cars is called Google Chauffeur. Lettering on the side of each car identifies it as a "self-driving car." The project is currently being led by Google engineer Sebastian Thrun, director of the Stanford Artificial Intelligence Laboratory and co-inventor of Google Street View. Thrun's team at Stanford created the robotic vehicle Stanley which won the 2005 DARPA Grand Challenge and its US $ 2 million prize from the United States Department of Defense. The team developing the system consisted of 15 engineers working for Google, including Chris Urmson, Mike Montemerlo, and Anthony Levandowski who had worked on the DARPA Grand and Urban Challenges.

The U.S. state of Nevada passed a law on June 29, 2011 permitting the operation of autonomous cars in Nevada. Google had been lobbying for robotic car laws. The Nevada law went into effect on March 1, 2012, and the Nevada Department of Motor Vehicles issued the first license for an autonomous car in May 2012. The license was issued to a Toyota Prius modified with Google's experimental driverless technology. As of April 2012, Florida became the second state to allow the testing of autonomous cars on public roads. California became the third state to legalize the use of self-driven cars for testing purposes as of September 2012 when Governor Jerry Brown signed the bill into law at Google HQ in Mountain View. Governor Rick Snyder signed legislation allowing the testing of automated or self-driving vehicles on Michigan's roads in December 2013, but requires a human in the driver seat at all time while the vehicle is in use.

1) Technology

Google's robotic cars have about $150,000 in equipment including a $70,000 LIDAR (laser radar) system. The range finder mounted on the top is a Velodyne 64-beam laser. This laser allows the vehicle to generate a detailed 3D map of its environment. The car then takes these generated maps and combines them with high-resolution maps of the world, producing different types of data models that allow it to drive itself.

2) Road Testing

The project team has equipped a test group of at least ten cars, consisting of six Toyota Prius, an Audi TT, and three Lexus RX450h (Figure 4.3), each accompanied in the driver's seat by one of a dozen drivers with unblemished driving records and in the passenger seat by one of Google's engineers. The car has traversed San Francisco's Lombard Street, famed for its steep hairpin turns and through city traffic. The vehicles have driven over the Golden Gate Bridge and around Lake Tahoe. The system drives at the speed limit it has stored on its maps and maintains its distance from other vehicles using its system of sensors. The system provides an override that allows a human driver to take control of

Figure 4.3 Lexus RX450h retrofitted as a Google driverless car

the car by stepping on the brake or turning the wheel, similar to cruise control systems already found in many cars today.

On March 28, 2012, Google posted a YouTube video showing Steve Mahan, a Morgan Hill California resident, being taken on a ride in its self-driving Toyota Prius. In the video, Mahan states "Ninety-five percent of my vision is gone, I'm well past legally blind". In the description of the YouTube video, it is noted that the carefully programmed route takes him from his home to a drive-through restaurant, then to the dry cleaning shop, and finally back home.

In August 2012, the team announced that they have completed over 300,000 autonomous-driving miles (500,000 km) accident-free, typically have about a dozen cars on the road at any given time, and are starting to test them with single drivers instead of in pairs. Four U.S. states have passed laws permitting autonomous cars as of December 2013: Nevada, Florida, California, and Michigan. A law proposed in Texas would establish criteria for allowing "autonomous motor vehicles".

3) Commercialization

While Google had no immediate plans to commercially develop the system, the company hopes to develop a business which would market the system and the data behind it to automobile manufacturers. An attorney for the California Department of Motor Vehicles raised concerns that "The technology is ahead of the law in many areas," citing state laws that "all presume to have a human being operating the vehicle". According to The New York Times, policy makers and regulators have argued that new laws will be required if driverless vehicles are to become a reality because "the technology is now advancing so quickly that it is in danger of outstripping existing law, some of which dates back to the era of horse-drawn carriages".

Google lobbied for two bills that made Nevada the first state where autonomous vehicles can be legally operated on public roads. The first bill is an amendment to an electric vehicle bill that provides for the licensing and testing of autonomous vehicles. The second bill will provide an exemption from the ban on distracted driving to permit occupants to send text messages while sitting behind the wheel. The two bills came to a vote before the Nevada state legislature's session ended in June 2011. It has been speculated that Nevada was selected due to the Las Vegas Auto Show and the Consumer Electronics Show, and the high likelihood that Google will present the first commercially viable product at either or both of these events. Google executives, however, refused to state the precise reason they chose Nevada to be the maiden state for the autonomous car.

Nevada passed a law in June 2011 concerning the operation of autonomous cars in Nevada, which went into effect on March 1, 2012. A Toyota Prius modified with Google's experimental driverless technology was licensed by the Nevada Department of Motor Vehicles (DMV) in May 2012. This was the first license issue in the United States for a self-driven car. License plates issued in Nevada for autonomous cars will have a red background and feature an infinity symbol (∞) on the left side because, according to the DMV Director, "... using the infinity symbol was the best way to represent the 'car of the future'." Nevada's regulations require a person behind the wheel and one in the passenger's seat during tests.

In August 2013 news reports surfaced about Robo-Taxi, a driverless vehicle from Google. These reports re-appeared again in early 2014, following the granting of a patent to Google for an advertising fee funded transportation service which including autonomous vehicles as a method of transport.

4.2.3 How Google's Self-driving Car Works

Once a secret project, Google's autonomous vehicles are now out in the open, quite literally, with the company test-driving them on public roads and, on one occasion, even inviting people to ride inside one of the robot cars as it raced around a closed course.

Google's fleet of robotic Toyota Priuses has now logged more than 190,000 miles (about 300,000 kilometers), driving in city traffic, busy highways, and mountainous roads with only occasional human intervention. The project is still far from becoming commercially viable, but

Google has set up a demonstration system on its campus, using driverless golf carts, which points to how the technology could change transportation even in the near future.

Stanford University professor Sebastian Thrun, who guides the project, and Google engineer Chris Urmson discussed these and other details in a keynote speech at the IEEE International Conference on Intelligent Robots and Systems in San Francisco last month.

Thrun and Urmson explained how the car works and showed videos of the road tests, including footage of what the on-board computer "sees" and how it detects other vehicles, pedestrians, and traffic lights (Figure 4.4).

Figure 4.4　Footage of what the on-board computer "sees"

Google has released details and videos of the project before, but this is the first time I have seen some of this footage—and it's impressive. It actually changed my views of the whole project, which I used to consider a bit far-fetched. Now I think this technology could really help to achieve some of the goals Thrun has in sight: Reducing road accidents, congestion, and fuel consumption.

Urmson, who is the tech lead for the project, said that the "heart of our system" is a laser range finder mounted on the roof of the car. The device, a Velodyne 64-beam laser, generates a detailed 3D map of the environment. The car then combines the laser measurements with high-resolution maps of the world, producing different types of data models that allow it to drive itself while avoiding obstacles and respecting traffic laws.

The vehicle also carries other sensors, which include: four radars, mounted on the front and rear bumpers, that allow the car to "see" far enough to be able to deal with fast traffic on freeways; a camera, positioned near the rear-view mirror, that detects traffic lights; and a GPS, inertial measurement unit, and wheel encoder, that determine the vehicle's location and keep track of its movements.

Here's a slide showing the different subsystems (Figure 4.5) and functions (Figure 4.6):

Two things seem particularly interesting about Google's approach. First, it relies on very detailed maps of the roads and terrain, something that Urmson said is essential to determine accurately where the car is. Using GPS-based techniques alone, he said, the location could be off by several meters.

The second thing is that, before sending the self-driving car on a road test, Google engineers drive along the route one or more times to gather data about the environment. When it's the autonomous vehicle's turn to drive itself, it compares the data it is acquiring to the previously recorded data, an approach that is useful to differentiate pedestrians from stationary objects like poles and mailboxes.

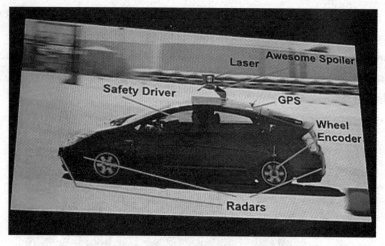

Figure 4.5 Sensors of Google's self-driving car

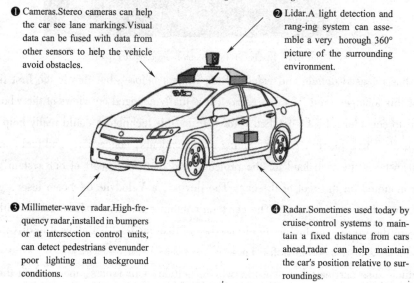

❶ Cameras.Stereo cameras can help the car see lane markings.Visual data can be fused with data from other sensors to help the vehicle avoid obstacles.

❷ Lidar.A light detection and rang-ing system can assemble a very horough 360° picture of the surrounding environment.

❸ Millimeter-wave radar.High-frequency radar,installed in bumpers or at intersection control units, can detect pedestrians evenunder poor lighting and background conditions.

❹ Radar.Sometimes used today by cruise-control systems to maintain a fixed distance from cars ahead,radar can help maintain the car's position relative to surroundings.

Figure 4.6 Functions of main sensors

At one point you can see the car stopping at an intersection. After the light turns green, the car starts a left turn, but there are pedestrians crossing (Figure 4.7). No problem: It yields to the pedestrians, and even to a guy who decides to cross at the last minute.

Sometimes, however, the car has to be more "aggressive". When going through a four-way intersection, for example, it yields to other vehicles based on road rules; but if other cars don't reciprocate, it advances a bit to show to the other drivers its intention. Without programming that kind of behavior, Urmson said, it would be impossible for the robot car to drive in the real world.

Clearly, the Google engineers are having a lot of fun (fast forward to 13:00 to see Urmson smiling broadly as the car speeds through Google's parking lot, the tires squealing at every turn).

But the project has a serious side. Thrun and his Google colleagues, including co-founders

Larry Page and Sergey Brin, are convinced that smarter vehicles could help make transportation safer and more efficient: Cars would drive closer to each other, making better use of the 80 percent to 90 percent of empty space on roads, and also form speedy convoys on freeways.

Figure 4.7　The car starts a left turn, but there are pedestrians crossing

They would react faster than humans to avoid accidents, potentially saving thousands of lives. Making vehicles smarter will require lots of computing power and data, and that's why it makes sense for Google to back the project, Thrun said in his keynote.

Urmson described another scenario they envision: Vehicles would become a shared resource, a service that people would use when needed. You'd just tap on your smartphone, and an autonomous car would show up where you are, ready to drive you anywhere. You'd just sit and relax or do work.

He said they put together a video showing a concept called Caddy Beta that demonstrates the idea of shared vehicles—in this case, a fleet of autonomous golf carts. He said the golf carts are much simpler than the Priuses in terms of on-board sensors and computers. In fact, the carts communicate with sensors in the environment to determined their location and "see" the incoming traffic.

"This is one way we see in the future this technology can... actually make transportation better, make it more efficient," Urmson said.

Thrun and Urmson acknowledged that there are many challenges ahead, including improving the reliability of the cars and addressing daunting legal and liability issues. But they are optimistic (Nevada recently became the first U. S. state to make self-driving cars legal.) All the problems of transportation that people see as a huge waste, "we see that as an opportunity," Thrun said.

New Words and Expressions

cusp[kʌsp]　　　　　　　　　　　　　　n. 尖端
affordable[ə'fɔː(r)dəb(ə)l]　　　　　　adj. 付得起的
revolutionary[ˌrevə'luːʃ(ə)n(ə)rɪ]　　　adj. 革命性的
attorney[ə'tɜː(r)nɪ]　　　　　　　　　　n. 代理人,律师
outstrip[ˌaʊt'strɪp]　　　　　　　　　　vt. 超过,优于

DARPA		美国国防部高级研究计划局
commercialization [kə͵mɜːʃəlaɪˈzeɪ(ə)n]	n.	商业化,商品化
policy makers and regulators		政策制定者和监管机构
legislature [ˈledʒɪslətʃə(r)]	n.	立法机构,议会
speculate [ˈspekjʊleɪt]	v.	思索,推测
occasional [əˈkeɪʒ(ə)nəl]	adj.	偶尔的,不经常的
on-board computer		车载计算机,车载电脑
congestion [kənˈdʒestʃ(ə)n]	n.	拥挤,堵车
bumpers [ˈbʌmpəz]	n.	保险杠
terrain [təˈreɪn]	n.	地形
gather [ˈɡæðə(r)]	v.	收集
reciprocate [rɪˈsɪprəkeɪt]	v.	呼唤,交互
convoy [ˈkɒnˌvɔɪ]	n.	车队
scenario [səˈnɑːrɪoʊ]	n.	场景,方案
daunting [ˈdɔːntɪŋ]	adj.	令人畏惧的,令人气馁的

Exercises

I. True or false

a) The license was issued to a Golf 7 modified with Google's experimental driverless technology.

b) Vehicles would become a shared resource, a service that people would use when needed.

c) Using GPS-based techniques alone, the location is without error.

d) Nevada's regulations don't require any person in the self-driving cars during tests.

e) Nevada recently became the first U.S. state to make self-driving cars legal.

II. Filling blanks

a) The software powering Google's cars is called _____.

b) _____ became the third state to legalize the use of self-driven cars for testing purposes as of September 2012.

c) The license was issued to a _____ modified with Google's experimental driverless technology.

d) _____ University professor Sebastian Thrun, who guides the project.

e) Thrun and Urmson acknowledged that there are many challenges ahead, including improving the _____ of the cars and addressing daunting legal and liability issues.

III. Translation

a) Now, in the early decades of the 21st century, the industry appears to be on the cusp of revolutionary change—with potential to dramatically reshape not just the competitive landscape but also the way we interact with vehicles and, indeed, the future design of our roads and cities. The revolution, when it comes, will be engendered by the advent of autonomous or "self-driving" vehicles. And the timing may be sooner than you think.

b) Nevada passed a law in June 2011 concerning the operation of autonomous cars in Nevada, which went into effect on March 1, 2012. A Toyota Prius modified with Google's experimental driverless technology was licensed by the Nevada Department of Motor Vehicles (DMV) in May 2012. This was the first license issue in the United States for a self-driven car.

c) The vehicle also carries other sensors, which include: four radars, mounted on the front and rear bumpers, that allow the car to "see" far enough to be able to deal with fast traffic on freeways; a camera, positioned near the rear-view mirror, that detects traffic lights; and a GPS, inertial measurement unit, and wheel encoder, that determine the vehicle's location and keep track of its movements.

4.3 Automatic Parking System

4.3.1 Automatic Parking-assist Systems

Parking-assist systems help drivers in avoiding the minor "dings" that can come with parking maneuvers. This is particularly true in urban areas in Europe and Japan in which parking spaces are very tight.

The simplest form of parking-assist system is a rear-facing video camera, which offers a view of the area behind the vehicle but no sensing or driver warnings. The video image is displayed on the driver's console screen, which otherwise acts as the navigation display when the vehicle is moving forward. Typically, the rearview image appears automatically on the screen when the vehicle is shifted into reverse gear. In this way, the driver can see small objects to the rear and assess distances to walls and obstacles.

Parking-assist sensor systems generally use ultrasonic sensing of the immediate area near the car, on the order of 1-2m. More advanced systems use radar to cover an extended range and provide the driver with more precise information as to the location of any obstacle. When combined with a rear-looking video display, calibrated scales can be overlaid on the screen to indicate to drivers the precise distance from an obstacle.

A fascinating form of advanced parking assist was recently introduced by Toyota, in which the complex steering maneuvers required for parallel parking are completely automated. When the driver shifts into reverse gear, a rearview video image is displayed. Overlaid on this image is a rectangle that is sized to represent the host vehicle. The driver uses arrow keys to position this rectangle over the desired parking space within the image. After a "set" key is pressed, the driver is instructed to proceed by operating the accelerator and brakes, while the system takes care of steering to maneuver the vehicle precisely into the parking space.

4.3.2 How Self-parking Cars Work

4.3.2.1 Introduction to How Self-parking Cars Work

Parallel parking is an ordeal for many drivers, but with parking space limited in big cities, squeezing your car into a tiny space is a vital skill. It's seldom an easy task, and it can lead to traffic tie-ups, frazzled nerves and bent fenders. Fortunately, technology has an answer—cars that park themselves. Imagine finding the perfect parking spot, but instead of struggling to maneuver

Figure 4.8 The British Toyota Prius with Intelligent Parking Assist has a dashboard screen to tell the driver what to do

your car back and forth, you simply press a button, sit back, and relax (Figure 4.8). The same technology used in self-parking cars can be used for collision avoidance systems and ultimately, self-driving cars.

Automakers are starting to market self-parking cars because they sense a consumer demand. Parallel parking is often the most feared part of the driver's test, and it's something almost everyone has to do at some point. People who live in big cities may have to do it every day. Removing the difficulty, stress and uncertainty of this chore is very appealing.

Self-parking cars can also help to solve some of the parking and traffic problems in dense urban areas. Sometimes parking a car in a space is restricted by the driver's skill at parallel parking. A self-parking car can fit into smaller spaces than most drivers can manage on their own. This makes it easier for people to find parking spaces, and allows the same number of cars to take up fewer spaces. When someone parallel parks, they often block a lane of traffic for at least a few seconds. If they have problems getting into the spot, this can last for several minutes and seriously disrupt traffic.

Finally, the difficulty of parallel parking leads to a lot of minor dents and scratches. Self-parking technology would prevent many of these mishaps. It can also save money, since you won't have to worry about insurance claims for parking-related damage.

4.3.2.2 Self-parking Technology

Self-parking technology is mostly used in parallel parking situations (although BMW has a prototype that parks itself in horizontal spaces, like small garages). Parallel parking requires cars to park parallel to a curb, in line with the other parked cars. Most people need about six feet more space than the total length of their car to successfully parallel park, although some expert drivers can do it with less space.

To parallel park, the driver must follow these five basic steps (Figure 4.9):

(1) He pulls ahead of the space and stops beside the car in front of it.

(2) Turning the car's wheels towards the curb, he backs into the space at around a 45-degree angle.

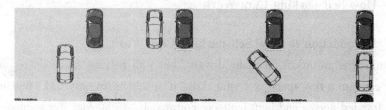

Figure 4.9 Parallel parking

(3) When his front wheels are even with the rear wheels of the car in front of him, he straightens them and continues backing up.

(4) While checking his rear view to be sure that he doesn't come too close to the car behind him, the driver turns his wheels away from the curb to swing the front end of his car into the space.

(5) Finally, the driver pulls forward and backwards in the space until his car is about one foot away from the curb.

Self-parking cars currently on the market are not completely autonomous, but they do make parallel parking much easier. The driver still regulates the speed of the vehicle by pressing and releasing the brake pedal (the car's idle speed is enough to move it into the parking space without pressing the gas pedal). Once the process begins, the on-board computer system take over the steering wheel.

The car moves forward into position beside the front car, and a signal lets the driver know when he should stop. Then the driver shifts the car into reverse and releases the brake slightly to begin moving backward. Using the power steering system, the computer turns the wheel and perfectly maneuvers the car into the parking space. When the car has backed far enough into the space, another signal lets the driver know that he should stop and shift the car into drive. The car pulls forward as the wheels adjust to maneuver it into the space. A final signal (on the British Toyota Prius, it's a female voice that intones, "The assist is finished.") tells the driver when parking is complete.

On the British Toyota Prius, a large computer screen mounted on the dashboard gives the driver notifications such as when to stop, when to shift into reverse, and when to slowly ease off the brake to move the car into the parking spot.

Different self-parking systems have different ways of sensing the objects around the car. Some have sensors distributed around the front and rear bumpers of the car, which act as both transmitters and receivers. These sensors transmit signals, which bounce off objects around the car and reflect back to them. The car's computer then uses the amount of time that it takes those signals to return to calculate the location of the objects. Others systems have cameras mounted onto the bumpers or use radar to detect objects. The end result is the same: the car detects the other parked cars, the size of the parking space and the distance to the curb, then steers it into the space.

Next, we'll look at the specific models on the market and what's in store for the future.

4.3.2.3 Future Self-parking Cars

In 1992, Volkswagen employed self-parking technology in its IRVW (Integrated Research Volkswagen) Futura concept car. The IRVW parked with full autonomy—the driver could get out of the car and watch as it parked itself. A PC-sized computer in the trunk controlled the system. Volkswagen estimated that this feature would've added about $3,000 to the price of a car, and it was never offered on a production model.

In 2003, Toyota began offering a self-parking option, called Intelligent Parking Assist, on its Japanese Prius hybrid. Three years later, British drivers had the option of adding self-parking to the Prius for the equivalent of $ 700 (Figure 4.10). So far, seventy percent of British Prius buyers have chosen this feature. Toyota plans to introduce the self-parking Prius to the United States in the near future, but no date has been set.

Figure 4.10   2006 Toyota Prius

Although Toyota is currently the only company with a self-parking car on the market, others have self-parking systems in the works. In 2004, a group of students at Linköping University in Sweden collaborated with Volvo on a project called Evolve. The Evolve car can parallel park autonomously. The students fitted a Volvo S60 with sensors and a computer in its trunk, which controls the steering wheel as well as the gas and brake pedals. Seimens VDO is working on a standalone driver assistance system called Park Mate, which would help drivers find a space as well as park in it (Figure 4.11).

A car that can take control of the wheel to park itself is one thing, but a self-driving car is another. It seems like a futurist's dream: millions of fuel-efficient cars driving smoothly under computer control, safely avoiding collisions and maintaining safe speeds, while the "drivers" sit back and watch TV or take a nap. How far are we from a "Jetsons"-like autotopia? Probably pretty far.

Many people enjoy driving, so it might be difficult for them to relinquish control of their vehicles to a computer, even if it would be safer. Product liability laws also have to be taken into account. However, the technology isn't far away. General Motors plans to offer a self-driving 2008 Opel Vectra to German drivers (Figure 4.12). The car will drive by itself at 60 mph, using a system of cameras, lasers and computers to track lanes, road signs, curves, obstacles and other cars.

Figure 4.11   Seimens VDO's Park Mate would help drivers find parking spots as well as park in them

Figure 4.12   The 2008 Opel Vectra at the Opel Zentrum in Berlin, Germany

Some cars already have a semi-automated cruise control system, known as adaptive cruise control. This system allows the driver to set a speed, just like regular cruise control. However, this system uses lasers to detect the distance to any vehicles on the road ahead, and automatically slows the car down if it gets too close.

Another upcoming development would use wireless technology to connect cars to each other. If one car detected slippery conditions on a curve, cars behind it would receive the information and slow down. Traction control systems would also kick into action. In addition, this system could detect traffic conditions by tracking the speeds of other cars and then suggest alternate routes.

While self-parking cars might seem like a frivolous luxury at the moment, they're actually the next step in the evolution of automotive technology. For lots more information about self-parking cars, car systems and related topics, check out the links on the next page.

New Words and Expressions

console [ˈkɑnˌsoʊl]	n. 控制台,操纵台,中控台
reverse gear	倒挡
ultrasonic [ˌʌltrəˈsɑnɪk]	n. 超声波
obstacle [ˈɑbstək(ə)l]	n. 障碍,障碍物
dashboard [ˈdæʃˌbɔː(r)d]	n. 仪表盘,挡泥板
ordeal [ɔː(r)ˈdiːl]	n. 严峻的考验,折磨
tie-up [ˈtaɪʌp]	n. 停泊处,停泊的场所;联合,关系
fender [ˈfendə(r)]	n. (车辆的)挡泥板
parallel parking	纵列式停车,侧向位停车
mishap [ˈmɪsˌhæp]	n. 灾祸;不幸事故
brake pedal	制动踏板
gas pedal	加速踏板
Linköping University	林雪平大学(瑞典)
alternate [ˈɔːltə(r)neɪt]	adj. 代替的,轮流的,交替的
frivolous [ˈfrɪv(ə)ləs]	adj. 无价值的,毫无意义的

Exercises

I. True or false

a) The simplest form of parking-assist system is a rear-facing video camera, which offers a view of the area behind the vehicle but no sensing or driver warnings.

b) Self-parking cars currently on the market are completely autonomous.

c) Parallel parking is often the easiest part of the driver's test.

d) BYD of CHINA is currently the only company with a self-parking car on the market.

e) Many people enjoy driving, so it might be difficult for them to relinquish control of their vehicles to a computer, even if it would be safer.

II. Filling blanks

a) Parking-assist sensor systems generally use _____ sensing of the immediate area near the car, on the order of 1-2m.

b) In 2003, Toyota began offering a self-parking option, called _____, on its Japanese Prius hybrid.

c) Seimens VDO is working on a standalone driver assistance system called _____, which would help drivers find a space as well as park in it.

d) A group of students at Linköping University in _____ collaborated with Volvo on a project called Evolve in 2004.

e) Another upcoming development would use _____ technology to connect cars to each other.

III. Translation

a) The simplest form of parking-assist system is a rear-facing video camera, which offers a view of the area behind the vehicle but no sensing or driver warnings. The video image is displayed on the driver's console screen, which otherwise acts as the navigation display when the vehicle is moving forward. Typically, the rearview image appears automatically on the screen when the vehicle is shifted into reverse gear. In this way, the driver can see small objects to the rear and assess distances to walls and obstacles.

b) Parallel parking is an ordeal for many drivers, but with parking space limited in big cities, squeezing your car into a tiny space is a vital skill. It's seldom an easy task, and it can lead to traffic tie-ups, frazzled nerves and bent fenders. Fortunately, technology has an answer—cars that park themselves. Imagine finding the perfect parking spot, but instead of struggling to maneuver your car back and forth, you simply press a button, sit back, and relax. The same technology used in self-parking cars can be used for collision avoidance systems and ultimately, self-driving cars.

c) Another upcoming development would use wireless technology to connect cars to each other. If one car detected slippery conditions on a curve, cars behind it would receive the information and slow down. Traction control systems would also kick into action. In addition, this system could detect traffic conditions by tracking the speeds of other cars and then suggest alternate routes.

Chapter 5 Advanced Public Transportation Systems(APTS)

5.1 Urban Transit Definitions

5.1.1 Definitions and Types of Urban Transit

Urban transit systems are the common carriers of passengers in cities. Urban transit is not a distinct technology, but an operational and institutional concept. It uses highway and railroad engineering extensively, as well as the operations and management methods employed by common carriers in any of the other transportation modes. Urban transit has great effect on the development of city politics and economy, culture and education, science and technology as well as other aspects, which is also an important aspect of the urban construction. Figure 5.1 shows Guo Mao overpass in Beijing. It's the intersection of the 3rd Ring Road and Chang'an Avenue.

Figure 5.1 Guo Mao overpass in Beijing

The urban transit development process has great differences around the world, which is affected by the national economy and the level of science and technology.

Urban transit system is a passenger service system, mainly includes bus, trolley bus, tram, light rail transit, subway and taxi etc. With the development of the city, railway suburban passenger transport has become an essential part.

In addition, in some river flowed city, the public transport system also comprises ferry. In the mountain city, cable and cable car transportation have been developing as well. Magnetic levitation passenger transportation and driverless taxi system is still on trial. Buses, trams, trolley buses, which are flexible and low-cost, are the main transportation tools in small and medium-sized cities in general. It's becoming the theme of urban public transportation.

Mass rapid public transport system including subway, light rail, high-speed railway, can carry large quantities of passengers quickly. It appears in some big cities, such as Shanghai, Beijing, Guangzhou, Wuhan, etc. It has the characteristics of large volume, high speed, high reliability, and can promote the formation of real estate development and commercial economic area, but the cost is very high, it is generally used as the skeleton of the city public transportation. Figure 5.2 shows Sui-Wan-Shen Intercity Rail. It's one of the main line of the Pearl River Delta intercity rail transit network planning.

Figure 5.2　Sui-Wan-Shen Intercity Rail

Auxiliary public transportation system including taxi, tricycle, motorcycle, bicycle, can meet the different requirements of passenger traveling. It plays a supplementary role in city public transportation.

Special public transportation system including ferries, tramway etc. is generally used in special conditions as this category of traffic is restraint by the geographical conditions.

In the modern big city, fast tram, metro system has gradually become the backbone of the city traffic.

Urban transit has the advantages of large capacity, high efficiency, low energy consumption, relatively less pollution and low transportation cost. They are particularly obvious on transportation trunks.

In some cities of China, some organizations provide shuttle buses for their staff to work. It has objectively become an auxiliary power for the urban transit.

5.1.2　Challenges of Urban Transit

Challenges facing urban transportation cities are locations having a high level of accumulation and concentration of economic activities and are complex spatial structures that are supported by transport systems.

The larger the city, the greater its complexity and the potential for disruptions, particularly when this complexity is not effectively managed. The most important transport problems are often related to urban areas and take place when transport systems, for a variety of reasons, cannot satisfy the numerous requirements of urban mobility. Urban productivity is highly dependent on the efficiency of its transport system to move labor, consumers and freight between multiple origins and destinations.

Additionally, important transport terminals such as ports, airports, and rail yards are located within urban areas, contributing to a specific array of problems. Some problems are ancient, like congestion (which plagued cities such as Rome), while others are new like urban freight distribution or environmental impacts. Among the most notable urban transport problems are:

- Traffic congestion and parking difficulties. Congestion is one of the most prevalent transport problems in large urban agglomerations, usually above a threshold of about 1 million inhabitants. It is particularly linked with motorization and the diffusion of the automobile, which has increased the demand for transport infrastructures. However, the supply of infrastructures has often not been able to keep up with the growth of mobility. Since vehicles spend the majority of the time parked, motorization has expanded the demand for parking space, which has created space consumption problems particularly in central areas; the spatial imprint of parked vehicles is significant. Congestion and parking are also interrelated since looking for a parking space (called "cruising") creates additional delays and impairs local circulation. In central areas of large cities cruising may account for more than 10% of the local circulation as drivers can spend 20 minutes looking for a parking spot. This practice is often judged more economically effective than using a paying off-street parking facility as the time spent looking for a free (or low cost) parking space as compensated by the monetary savings. Also, many delivery vehicles will simply double-park at the closest possible spot to unload their cargo.

- Longer commuting. On par with congestion people are spending an increasing amount of time commuting between their residence and workplace. An important factor behind this trend is related to residential affordability as housing located further away from central areas (where most of the employment remains) is more affordable. Therefore, commuters are trading time for housing affordability. However, long commuting is linked with several social problems, such as isolation, as well as poorer health (obesity).

- Public transport inadequacy. Many public transit systems, or parts of them, are either over or under used. During peak hours, crowdedness creates discomfort for users as the system copes with a temporary surge in demand. Low ridership makes many services financially unsustainable, particularly in suburban areas. In spite of significant subsidies and cross-financing (e.g. tolls) almost every public transit systems cannot generate sufficient income to cover its operating and capital costs. While in the past deficits were deemed acceptable because of the essential service public transit was providing for urban mobility, its financial burden is increasingly controversial.

- Difficulties for non-motorized transport. These difficulties are either the outcome of intense traffic, where the mobility of pedestrians, bicycles and vehicles is impaired, but also because of a blatant lack of consideration for pedestrians and bicycles in the physical design of infrastructures and facilities.

- Loss of public space. The majority of roads are publicly owned and free of access. Increased traffic has adverse impacts on public activities which once crowded the streets such as markets, agoras, parades and processions, games, and community interactions. These have gradually disappeared to be replaced by automobiles. In many cases, these activities have shifted to shopping malls while in other cases, they have been abandoned altogether. Traffic flows influence the life and interactions of residents and their usage of street space. More traffic impedes social interactions and street activities. People tend to walk and cycle less when traffic is high.

- Environmental impacts and energy consumption. Pollution, including noise, generated by circulation has become a serious impediment to the quality of life and even the health of urban populations. Further, energy consumption by urban transportation has dramatically increased and so the dependency on petroleum. Yet, peak oil considerations are increasingly linked with peak mobility expectations where high energy prices incite a shift towards more efficient and sustainable forms of urban transportation, namely public transit.

- Accidents and safety. Growing traffic in urban areas is linked with a growing number of accidents and fatalities, especially in developing countries. Accidents account for a significant share of recurring delays. As traffic increases, people feel less safe to use the streets.

- Land consumption. The territorial imprint of transportation is significant, particularly for the automobile. Between 30% and 60% of a metropolitan area may be devoted to transportation, an outcome of the over-reliance on some forms of urban transportation. Yet, this land consumption also underlines the strategic importance of transportation in the economic and social welfare of cities.

- Freight distribution. Globalization and the materialization of the economy have resulted in growing quantities of freight moving within cities. As freight traffic commonly shares infrastructures with the circulation of passengers, the mobility of freight in urban areas has become increasingly problematic. City logistics strategies can be established to mitigate the variety of challenges faced by urban freight distribution.

New Words and Expressions

urban transit	城市公共运输
carrier['kærɪə]	n. 运输公司,承运人
distinct[dɪ'stɪŋkt]	adj. 不同的
operational[ˌɔpə'reɪʃənl]	adj. 操作上的
institutional[ˌɪnstɪ'tjuːʃənl]	adj. 制度上的
highway['haɪweɪ]	n. 公路
extensively[ɪk'stensɪvlɪ]	adv. 广泛的
railroad['reɪlrəʊd]	n. 铁路,铁路运输
affect[ə'fekt]	vt. 影响
economy[ɪ'kɔnəmɪ]	n. 经济
trolley bus	无轨电车
tram[træm]	n. 有轨电车
light rail transit	轻轨
railway suburban passenger transport	铁路市郊旅客运输
in addition	另外
river flowed	河湖流经
comprise[kəm'praɪz]	vt. 包含,由……构成
ferry['ferɪ]	n. 轮渡
cable car	索道车

magnetic levitation passenger transportation	磁悬浮客运交通
theme [θi:m]	n. 主题
on trial	试行
flexible ['fleksəbl]	adj. 灵活的
in general	一般来说，通常
driverless taxi system	无人驾驶出租客运系统
mass rapid public transport system	快速大运量公共交通系统
skeleton ['skelɪtn]	n. 骨架
Sui-Wan-Shen Intercity Rail	穗莞深城际轨道
Pearl River Delta	珠江三角洲
commercial [kə'mɜ:ʃəl]	adj. 商业的
real estate	不动产
shuttle bus	班车
supplementary [ˌsʌplɪ'mentrɪ]	adj. 补充的
backbone ['bækbəʊn]	n. 脊椎；支柱
consumption [kən'sʌmpʃn]	n. 消费
relatively ['relətɪvlɪ]	adv. 相对地
transportation trunks	交通干线
auxiliary [ɔ:g'zɪlɪərɪ]	adj. 辅助的
accumulation [əˌkju:mjə'lɪʃn]	n. 积累
concentration [ˌkɔnsn'treɪʃn]	n. 集中
spatial ['speɪʃl]	adj. 空间的
agglomeration [əˌglɔmə'reɪʃn]	n. 群，成团
diffusion [dɪ'fju:ʒn]	n. 扩散

Exercises

I. True or false

a) Urban transit system is a passenger service system, mainly includes bus, trolley bus, tram, light rail transit, subway and taxi etc.

b) In addition, in some inland city, the public transport system also comprises ferry.

c) Mass rapid public transport system including subway, light rail, high-speed railway, can carry large quantities of passengers quickly.

d) In the modern big city, light rail, metro system has gradually become the backbone of the city traffic.

e) Special public transportation system including ferries, tramway etc. is generally used in special conditions.

II. Filling blanks

a) Urban transit has great effect on the development of city politics and economy, _____, science and technology as well as other aspects.

b) With the development of the city, _____ has become an essential part.

c) Magnetic levitation passenger transportation and _____ is still on trial.

d) Urban transit has the advantages of _____, high efficiency, _____, relatively less pollution and low transportation cost.

e) In some cities of China, some organizations provide _____ for their staff to work.

III. Translation

a) Urban transit systems are the common carriers of passengers in cities.

b) The urban transit development process has great differences around the world, which is affected by the national economy and the level of science and technology.

c) Buses, trams, trolley buses, which are flexible and low-cost, are the main transportation tools in small and medium-sized cities in general.

5.2 Public Transportation Priority

Bus rapid transit (BRT, BRTS) is a bus-based mass transit system. A true BRT system generally has specialized design, services and infrastructure to improve system quality and remove the typical causes of bus delay. Sometimes described as a "surface subway", BRT aims to combine the capacity and speed of a light rail or metro system with the flexibility, cost and simplicity of a bus system.

To be considered BRT, buses should operate for a significant part of their journey within a fully dedicated right of way (busway), in order to avoid traffic congestion. In addition, a true BRT system will have most of the following elements:

• a bus way alignment in the center of the road (to avoid typical curb-side delays);

• stations with off-board fare collection (to reduce boarding and alighting delay related to paying the driver);

• station platforms level with the bus floor (to reduce boarding and alighting delay caused by steps);

• bus priority at intersections (to avoid intersection signal delay).

In 2011, a BRT Standard Technical Committee was formed, and in 2013 it sets a minimum definition of what features must be part of a system to qualify as BRT. Figure 5.3 shows BRT Line 1 in Beijing. The speed of the buses should not fall below 25 km/h; the one-way passenger transportation capacity should reach between 10,000 and 15,000 people per hour.

Figure 5.3 BRT Line 1 in Beijing

5.2.1 Main Features

BRT systems normally include most of the following features:

• Dedicated lanes. Bus-only lanes make for faster travel and ensure that buses are never delayed due to mixed traffic congestion. Separate rights of way may be elevated, depressed, or routed through a tunnel, possibly using former rail routes. Transit malls or "bus streets" may also be created in city centers.

- Bus way alignment. Center of roadway or bus-only corridor keeps buses away from the busy curb-side, where cars and trucks are parking, standing and turning.

- Off-board fare collection. Fare payment at the station, instead of on board the bus, eliminates the delay caused by passengers waiting to pay on board.

- Intersection treatment. Prohibiting turns for traffic across the bus lane significantly reduces delays to the buses. In addition, bus priority will often be provided at signalized intersections to reduce delays by extending the green phase or reducing the red phase in the required direction compared to the normal sequence. However, prohibiting turns is the most important measure for moving buses through intersections—more important even than signal priority.

- Platform-level boarding. Station platform is at level with bus for quick and easy boarding, making it fully accessible for wheelchairs, disabled passengers, and baby strollers with minimal delays.

High-level platforms with high level buses makes it difficult to have stops outside dedicated platforms, and to have normal buses stop at high-level platforms, causing the BRT stops to be fully separated from other bus stops. In contrast to rail-bound traffic there is also a high risk of a dangerous gap between bus and platform.

An increasing popular variant are low-floor buses without steps at the door, which can allow easy boarding and have stops compatible with other buses. Figure 5.4 shows a BRT station on the Guangzhou Bus Rapid Transit system, which opened in 2010 and carries over 1,000,000 people per day.

Figure 5.4　A BRT station on the Guangzhou Bus Rapid Transit system

5.2.2　Additional Amenities

- High frequency all day service. A BRT network with comprehensive coverage can serve a diverse market (all income ranges) by moving large numbers of people between locations quickly and reliably throughout the day, while maintaining a comfortable riding experience. These characteristics are essential to satisfying the demands of a diverse market or offering high-frequency service without heavy subsidy.

- High capacity vehicles. High capacity vehicles, such bi-articulated buses may be used, which are typically fitted with multiple doors to speed entry and exit. Double-decker buses or Guided buses may also be used. Advanced powertrain control may be used for a smoother ride.

- Quality stations. BRT systems typically feature significant investment in enclosed stations which may incorporate attractive sliding glass doors, staffed ticket booths, information booths, and other more standard features listed above. They will often include level boarding, using either low-floor buses or higher boarding platforms level, and multiple doors to speed passenger boarding and enhance accessibility to disabled passengers. Validation of ticket upon entry to the "station" rather than boarding the bus in a similar manner to that used on entry to a subway system is also common, particularly at busy stations.

• Prominent brand or identity. Large cities usually have big bus networks. A map showing all bus lines might be incomprehensible and cause people to wait for low frequency buses. By branding a number of main bus lines having high frequency, with a special brand and separate maps, it is easier to understand the main network.

New Words and Expressions

priority [praɪˈɔrətɪ]	n.	优先权
bus rapid transit		快速公交
mass transit		公共交通;大量客运
delay [dɪˈleɪ]	n.	延迟;耽搁
surface [ˈsɔːfɪs]	n.	表面;地面
combine [kəmˈbaɪn]	vt.	使结合
simplicity [sɪmˈplɪsətɪ]	n.	简单
significant [sɪɡˈnɪfɪkənt]	adj.	重要的;有重大意义的
dedicated [ˈdedɪkeɪtɪd]	adj.	专用的
right of way		公交专用车道;通行权
avoid [əˈvɔɪd]	vt.	避免
congestion [kənˈdʒestʃən]	n.	拥挤;堵车;充血
element [ˈelɪmənt]	n.	要素
alignment [əˈlaɪnmənt]	n.	队列
typical [ˈtɪpɪkl]	adj.	典型的
curb-side		路边的
intersection [ˌɪntəˈsekʃn]	n.	交叉点;十字路口
feature [ˈfiːtʃə]	n.	特征
lane [leɪn]	n.	车道
ensure [ɪnˈʃʊə]	vt.	确保
due to		由于
elevated [ˈelɪveɪtɪd]	adj.	升高的
depressed [dɪˈprest]	adj.	下陷的
routed [ruːtɪd]	adj.	按照规定路线的
transit mall		换乘大厅
corridor [ˈkɔrɪdɔː]	n.	通道
keep away from		远离
eliminate [ɪˈlɪmɪneɪt]	vt.	排除;消除
prohibit [prəˈhɪbɪt]	vt.	禁止

phase [feɪz]	n. 周期
sequence [ˈsiːkwəns]	n. 顺序
accessible [əkˈsesəbl]	adj. 易使用的
in contrast to	相比之下
rail-bound	轨道
variant [ˈveəriənt]	n. 变化形式
compatible [kəmˈpætəbl]	adj. 兼容的
amenity [əˈminətɪ]	n. 便利
Double-decker	双层车
Guided buses	导游观光车

Exercises

I. True or false

a) Bus-only lanes make for slower travel and ensure that buses are never delayed due to mixed traffic congestion.

b) Prohibiting turns is not an important measure for moving buses through intersections.

c) High-level platforms with high level buses makes it difficult to have stops outside dedicated platforms.

d) Bus priority will often be provided at signalized intersections to reduce delays by extending the green phase or reducing the red phase in the required direction compared to the normal sequence.

e) An increasing popular variant are low-floor buses without steps at the door, which can allow easy boarding and have stops compatible with other buses.

II. Filling blanks

a) BRT aims to combine the _____ and _____ of a light rail or metro system with the flexibility, cost and simplicity of a bus system.

b) _____ may be elevated, depressed, or routed through a tunnel, possibly using former rail routes.

c) Fare payment at the station, instead of _____, eliminates the delay caused by passengers waiting to pay on board.

d) A true BRT system generally has _____, services and infrastructure to improve system quality and remove the typical causes of bus delay.

e) To be considered BRT, buses should operate for a significant part of their journey within a fully dedicated right of way (busway), in order to avoid _____.

III. Translation

a) Bus rapid transit (BRT, BRTS) is a bus-based mass transit system.

b) Prohibiting turns is the most important measure for moving buses through intersections—more important even than signal priority.

c) Station platform is at level with bus for quick and easy boarding, making it fully accessible for wheelchairs, disabled passengers, and baby strollers with minimal delays.

5.3 Automatic Vehicle Location

5.3.1 Definition

Automatic vehicle location (AVL) is a mean for automatically determining and transmitting the geographic location of a vehicle. This data, from one or more vehicles, may then be collected by a vehicle tracking system for a picture of vehicle travel.

Figure 5.5   GPS satellite

Most commonly, the location is determined using GPS, and the transmission mechanism is SMS, GPRS, a satellite (Figure 5.5 shows a GPS satellite) or terrestrial radio from the vehicle to a radio receiver. GSM and EVDO are the most common services applied, because of the low data rate needed for AVL, and the low cost and near-ubiquitous nature of these public networks. The low bandwidth requirements also allow for satellite technology to receive telemetry data at a moderately higher cost, but across a global coverage area and into very remote locations not covered well by terrestrial radio or public carriers. Other options for determining actual location, for example in environments where GPS illumination is poor, are dead reckoning, i.e. inertial navigation, or active RFID systems or cooperative RTLS systems. With advantage, combinations of these systems may be applied. In addition, terrestrial radio positioning systems utilizing an LF (Low Frequency) switched packet radio network were also used as an alternative to GPS based systems.

5.3.2 Applications

• Application with vehicles. Automatic vehicle locating is a powerful concept for managing fleets of vehicles, as service vehicles, emergency vehicles, and especially precious construction equipment, also public transport vehicles (buses and trains). It is also used to track mobile assets, such as non-wheeled construction equipment, non-motorized trailers, and mobile power generators.

• Application with vehicle drivers and crews. The other purpose of tracking is to provide graded service or to manage a large driver and crewing staff effectively. For example, suppose an ambulance fleet has an objective of arriving at the location of a call for service within six minutes of receiving the request. Using an AVL system allows evaluating the locations of all vehicles in service with driver and other crew in order to pick the vehicle that will most likely arrive at the destination fastest, (meeting the service objective).

5.3.3 Special Applications of Automatic Vehicle Locating

Vehicle location technologies can be used in the following scenarios:

- Fleet management: when managing a fleet of vehicles, knowing the real-time location of all drivers allows management to meet customer needs more efficiently. Vehicle location information can also be used to verify that legal requirements are being met, for example, those drivers are taking rest breaks and obeying speed limits.
- Passenger Information: Real-time Passenger information systems use predictions based on AVL input to show the expected arrival and departure times of Public Transport services.
- Asset tracking: companies needing to track valuable assets for insurance or other monitoring purposes can now plot the real-time asset location on a map and closely monitor movement and operating status. For example, haulage and logistics companies often operate trucks with detachable load carrying units. In this case, trailers can be tracked independently of the cabs used to drive them. Combining vehicle location with inventory management that can be used to reconcile which item is currently on which vehicle can be used to identify physical location down to the level of individual packages.
- Field worker management: companies with a field service or sales workforce can use information from vehicle tracking systems to plan field workers' time, schedule subsequent customer visits and be able to operate these departments efficiently.
- Covert surveillance: vehicle location devices attached covertly by law enforcement or espionage organizations can be used to track journeys made by individuals who are under surveillance.

5.3.4 Difference between AVL and Events Activated Tracking Systems

It might be helpful to draw a distinction between vehicle location systems which track automatically and event activated tracking systems which track when triggered by an event. There is increasingly crossover between the different systems and those with experience of this sector will be able to draw on a number of examples which break the rule.

AVL (Automatic Vehicle Location). This type of vehicle tracking is normally used in the fleet or driver management sector. The unit is configured to automatically transmit its location at a set time interval, e.g. every 5 minutes. The unit is activated when the ignition is switched on/off.

EATS (Events Activated Tracking system). This type of system is primarily used in connection with vehicle or driver security solutions. If, for example a thief breaks into your car and attempts to steal it, the tracking system can be triggered by the immobilizer unit or motion sensor being activated. A monitoring bureau, will then be automatically notified that the unit has been activated and begin tracking the vehicle.

Some products on the market are a hybrid of both AVL and EATS technology. However industry practice has tended to lean towards a separation of these functions. It is worth taking note that vehicle tracking products tend to fall into one, not both of the technologies.

AVL technology is predominately used when applying vehicle tracking to fleet or driver management solutions. The use of Automatic Vehicle Location is given in the following scenario; a car breaks down by the side of the road and the occupant calls a vehicle recovery company. The vehicle recovery company has several vehicles operating in the area. Without needing to call each driver to check his location the dispatcher can pinpoint the nearest recovery vehicle and assign it to the new job. If you were to incorporate the other aspects of vehicle telematics into this scenario; the dispatcher, rather than phoning the recovery vehicle operative, could transmit the job details directly to the operative's mobile data device, which would then use the in-vehicle satellite navigation to aid his journey to the job.

EATS technology is predominately used when applying vehicle tracking to vehicle security solutions. An example of this distinction is given in the following scenario: A construction company owns some pieces of plant machinery that are regularly left unattended, at weekends, on building sites. Thieves break onto one site and piece equipment, such as a digger, is loaded on the back of a flatbed truck and then driven away. Typically the ignition wouldn't need to be turned on and as such most of the AVL products available wouldn't typically be activated. Only products that included a unit that was activated by a motion sensor or Geo Fence alarm event would be activated.

Both AVL and EATS systems track, but often for different purposes.

New Words and Expressions

Automatic vehicle Location (AVL)	自动车辆定位
determine [dɪˈtəːmɪn]	v. 做决定
transit [ˈtrænzɪt]	v. 传输
geographic [ˌdʒiːəˈɡræfɪk]	adj. 地理的
vehicle tracking system	车辆跟踪系统
GPS (Global Position System)	全球定位系统
SMS (Short Message Service)	短信服务
GPRS (General Packet Radio Service)	通用分组无线业务
terrestrial [təˈrestrɪəl]	adj. 陆地的；地球的
GSM (Global System for Mobile Communication)	全球移动通信系统
EVDO (Evolution Data Only)	高速数据传输服务
ubiquitous [juːˈbɪkwɪtəs]	adj. 无处不在的
bandwidth [ˈbændwɪdθ]	n. 带宽
moderately [ˈmɔdərətlɪ]	adv. 适度地
illumination [ɪˌluːmɪˈneɪʃn]	n. 阐明；解释
dead reckon	航位推测
inertial navigation	惯性导航
RFID (Radio Frequency Identification)	无线射频识别
RTLS (Real Time Location Systems)	实时定位系统
fleets of vehicles	车队的车辆
scenario [sɪˈneərɪˌəʊ]	n. 可能发生的情况
verify [ˈverɪfaɪ]	vt. 核实；证明
legal [ˈliːɡl]	adj. 合法的；法定的
obey [əˈbeɪ]	vt. 服从

real-time		实时
prediction[prɪˈdɪkʃn]	n.	预测
asset tracking		资产跟踪
plot[plɒt]	vt.	以图表画出
haulage[ˈhɔːlɪdʒ]	n.	公路货运业
logistics[ləˈdʒɪstɪks]	n.	物流
detachable[dɪˈtætʃəbl]	adj.	可分开的
trailer[ˈtreɪlə]	n.	拖车
inventory[ˈɪnvəntrɪ]	n.	库存
reconcile[ˈrekənsaɪl]	vt.	调和
convert[kənˈvɜːt]	vt.	(使)转变
enforcement[ɪnˈfɔːsmənt]	n.	强制
espionage[ˈespɪənɑːʒ]	n.	侦查;间谍活动
Events Activated Tracking system		活性追踪系统
Geo Fence		地理围栏
ignition[ɪgˈnɪʃn]	n.	点火器
hybrid[ˈhaɪbrɪd]	n.	混合物

Exercises

I. True or false

a) GPRS and EVDO are the most common services applied, because of the low data rate needed for AVL, and the low cost and near-ubiquitous nature of these public networks.

b) It is also used to track mobile assets, such as non-wheeled construction equipment, non-motorized trailers, and mobile power generators.

c) Using an AVL system allows evaluating the locations of all vehicles in service with driver and other crew.

d) Vehicle location information can also be used to verify that legal requirements are being met.

e) Companies with a field service or sales workforce can use information from vehicle tracking systems to plan field workers' time.

II. Filling blanks

a) This data, from one or more vehicles, may then be collected by a _____ for a picture of vehicle travel.

b) The location is determined using GPS, and the transmission mechanism is _____, _____, a satellite or terrestrial radio from the vehicle to a radio receiver.

c) The low _____ requirements also allow for satellite technology to receive telemetry data at a moderately higher cost.

d) The other purpose of tracking is to provide _____ or to manage a large driver and crewing staff effectively.

e) Real-time _____ use predictions based on AVL input to show the expected arrival and departure times of public transport services.

III. Translation

a) Automatic vehicle location is a mean for automatically determining and transmitting the geographic location of a vehicle.

b) Automatic vehicle locating is a powerful concept for managing fleets of vehicles, as service vehicles, emergency vehicles, and especially precious construction equipment, also public transport vehicles (buses and trains).

c) When managing a fleet of vehicles, knowing the real-time location of all drivers allows management to meet customer needs more efficiently.

Chapter 6 Commercial Vehicle Operation Systems(CVOS)

6.1 Intelligence in Transport Logistics

Since logistics advanced from 1950s, there were numerous researches focused on this area in different applications. Due to the trend of nationalization and globalization in recent decades, the importance of logistics management has been growing in various areas. For industries, logistics helps to optimize the existing production and distribution processes based on the same resources through management techniques for promoting the efficiency and competitiveness of enterprises. The key element in a logistics chain is transportation system, which joints the separated activities. Transportation occupies one-third of the amount in the logistics costs and transportation systems influence the performance of logistics system hugely. Transporting is required in the whole production procedures, from manufacturing to delivery to the final consumers and returns. Only a good coordination between each component would bring the benefits to a maximum.

6.1.1 Definition of Logistics

In 1991, Council of Logistics Management defined that logistics was part of the supply chain process that plans, implements, and controls the efficient, effective forward and reverse flow and storage of goods, services, and related information between the point of origin and the point of consumption in order to meet customers' requirements. In this definition, five important key terms, which are logistics, inbound logistics, materials management, physical distribution, and supply-chain management, are used to interpret. Logistics describes the entire process of materials and products moving into, through, and out of firm. Inbound logistics covers the movement of material received from suppliers. Materials management describes the movement of materials and components within a firm. Physical distribution refers to the movement of goods outward from the end of the assembly line to the customer. Finally, supply-chain management is somewhat larger than logistics, and it links logistics more directly with the user's total communications network and with the firm's engineering staff.

The commonality of the recent definitions is that logistics is a process of moving and handling goods and materials, from the beginning to the end of the production, sale process and waste disposal, to satisfy customers and add business competitiveness. It is the process of anticipating customer needs and wants; acquiring the capital, materials, people, technologies, and information necessary to meet those needs and wants; optimizing the goods- or service-producing network to fulfill customer requests; and utilizing the network to fulfill customer requests in a timely way. Simply to say, logistics is customer-oriented operation management.

6.1.2 Advancement of Logistics in ITS

In the 1970s and 1980s, information technologies such as LANs (Local Area Networks) and WANs (Wide Area Networks) were introduced to manage links and nodes in an isolated manner. As Just-In-Time management became prevalent in manufacturing, it called for Total Quality Management (TQM) which integrated logistics into other corporate functions. Thereby, link and node management became part of the overall management approach using innovative information network technologies. However, up to this stage, one corporation largely controlled the information networks.

In the 1990s, TQM evolved into logistics and at the same time the Internet revolution came to fruition. The need to manage door-to-door deliveries efficiently on a global scale prompted the expansion of corporate information networks to include suppliers, dealers, partners, subsidiaries and alliances in an integrated manner. The necessary integration of logistics operations across the supply chain has been made possible by the advancement of information technology.

Internet is rapidly becoming a powerful business tool because of its online commercial services and e-commerce capabilities. The net is ready to become a medium by which companies trade, make contracts, exchange data and information, discuss designs and locate components.

The application of information and communication technology (ICT) to transportation has also led to the emergence of Intelligent Transportation Systems (ITS).

The core of ITS consists in obtaining, processing, and distributing information for better use of the transportation system, infrastructure and services. It is traditional to examine Freight ITS according to the scope of the Commercial Vehicle Operation Systems (CVOS) for system-wide, regional, national, or continental applications and dedicated to the operations of a particular (group of) firm(s). Although different in scope, all systems require a number of enabling technologies, some of which are already firmly established, while others are still emerging. Most of these technologies also enable the e-business activities of the firm.

It is important to remember that the ITS idea is not a brand new concept emerging suddenly, but rather a logical evolution of transportation management drawing on old and new technologies. What is new about ITS is the vision of a globally integrated framework realizing a synergy between previously isolated systems. The rapid and concurrent development of electronic exchanges and partnerships is exacerbating the integration requirements.

Integration for ITS and e-business alike is not a simple task, however, as it must engage with a large array of disparate entities covering three broad areas: technical, political, and geographical. At the technical level, ITS bring together the fields of transportation planning, telecommunications, computing, vehicle and electronics manufacturing, and infrastructure construction. Many stakeholders are involved in the development, deployment, and operation of ITS: government agencies at the national, regional, and municipal levels, highway operators, carriers, equipment manufacturers, system vendors, service operators, etc. They must all collaborate to implement and run a system that is composed of a mixture of public and private assets, means and services. A geographical integration must also be achieved at regional and, in many cases, international levels. An end user, a container carrier for example, would not like to be forced to buy a different set of equipment for each city or country it intends to travel to. ITS are all about mobility, they are not meant to infringe on it. The efforts aimed at the development of standards and national architectures attempt to address these issues.

The continuity in the ITS evolution is illustrated by the strong relations between Electronic Data Interchange (EDI) and freight transportation. One may argue, in fact, that the common ancestor to CVOS developments is the adoption by the freight-transportation industry of EDI, two-way communication, and vehicle (and cargo) location and tracking technologies. This area of development is still going strong.

One can define EDI as the inter-organization, computer-to-computer exchange of business documentation in a standard, machine processable format. Its popularity has grown rapidly due to customer (shipper or large carrier) requirements as well as to several benefits associated with its use: minimization of manual data entry, increased transaction speed and accuracy, lower communication costs, and simplification of procedures. Major shippers (e.g., the auto industry), large carriers (e.g., railways) or infrastructure managers (port authorities) have initially promoted the utilization of EDI in the transportation industry, and they continue to be among the heaviest users of the technology. Smaller carriers followed, motivated mainly by the need to increase customer service and remain competitive. Pre-clearance activities in CVOS-equipped corridors or regions and at maritime and land border crossings require the utilization of EDI for information transmission among shippers, carriers, and officials. EDI supports CVOS not only to enable communications between dispatchers in control centers and vehicle operators in the field, but also to ensure timely and correct data delivery to the planning and monitoring systems of the firm. This reinforces the observations that there has to be a critical mass of EDI users in the market before it is financially justifiable, and that investing in technologies such as EDI may only be profitable when they are fully integrated with other systems within the organization.

The continuous improvement and integration of Global Positioning Systems (GPS) and communication technologies resulted in the improvement of their quality (up) and prices (down). This means wider acceptance of these technologies and their utilization in many modal and intermodal settings. The current focus of Information Technologies (IT) development is on wireless communications, the use of Internet, and the integration of the various technologies and data.

EDI, GPS, Automatic Identification Systems and similar technologies are also playing a continuously central role in freight terminals with a significant impact on the performance of transportation systems, particularly intermodal transportation, and logistic chains. Progress has been accomplished in introducing automation and advanced information and (some) decision technologies to freight terminals, port container terminals in particular. Considerable efforts are still being undertaken, while many innovative projects are proposed around the world. These developments are paralleled by an international effort to agree on standards for EDI exchanges not only for the transportation industry, but also for the whole range of logistics and supply chain activities.

The procedures related to logistics and intermodal transports are complex and often cumbersome, particularly at the international level. At work are numerous interactions between different parties with different objectives and operation policies. If intermodal transportation and supply chains are to operate efficiently and effectively, the relationships, actions, and terms used by the different participants must be understood by all. Efficiency and accountability require the seamless exchange of accurate, complete, and timely data among stakeholders. This requirement is further heightened by the growing understanding of needs for security of transport information, and for transfer of information related to security against terrorism, illegal immigration, as well as theft and traditional contraband. Several international organizations and committees focus on these issues for various types of transportation-related activities.

It is remarkable that EDI was one of the strongest initial enabling factors of partnerships and alliances between large numbers of carriers and shippers, before "electronic commerce" became a household name. This trend is actually leading to the electronic integration of carriers, operators of intermodal transfer facilities, and shippers with common interests in the movement of certain commodity groups or the utilization of particular infrastructures. Information technologies and appropriate planning and operating management methods and instruments are required to support and enhance such virtual business-to-business communities of interest.

6.1.3 Commercial Vehicle Operation Systems (CVOS)

CVOS, the applications of ITS for trucks, would be purchased by the managers of a trucking company. They would have a satellite navigation system, a small computer and a digital radio in each truck. Every fifteen minutes the computer transmits where the truck has been. The digital radio service forwards the data to the central office of the trucking company. A computer system in the central office manages the fleet in real time under control of a team of dispatchers.

In this way, the central office knows where its trucks are. The company tracks individual loads by using barcoded containers and pallets to track loads combined into a larger container. To minimize handling-expense, damage and waste of vehicle capacity, optimal-sized pallets are often constructed at distribution points to go to particular destinations.

A good load-tracking system will help deliver more than 95% of its loads via truck, on planned schedules. If a truck gets off its route, or is delayed, the truck can be diverted to a better route, or urgent loads that are likely to be late can be diverted to air freight. This allows a trucking company to deliver a true premium service at only slightly higher cost. The best proprietary systems, such as those operated by UPS, FedEx, TNT, and DHL, achieve better than 99.999% on-time delivery.

The well-managed CVOS provide drivers with huge amounts of help. They give them a view of their own load and the network of roadways.

CVOS could be summarized into 9 groups listed at below:
• Traffic controlling and monitoring systems: Such systems are created for controlling and managing the traffic flow by providing information regarding the traffic situation, such as colli-

sions, congestion, traffic flow speed and vehicles on the roads to be used by the authorities or by the logistics service providers. Such information is used for controlling the safety and security of transportation operations. Different technologies such as smart traffic lights, plate recognition cameras and speed measuring cameras equipped with sensors and variable traffic signs are used in such information systems. Such systems might affect the resource planning and management of the vehicles by increasing the safety and efficiency of the transportation operations. By using such systems the actors can send updates about their arrival time or delay notifications that lead to supporting efficiency of the truck, ports and terminal operations. The environmental performance of the transportation operations is increased by decreasing the transportation time and leads to having a more harmonized traffic flow.

• Weight-In-Motion (WIM) systems: Such systems are created for controlling and measuring the weight of the vehicles to increase safety of transportation and to decrease the damages caused by the over-weights. Weight-In-Motion systems can lead to improvement of performance by eliminating the stop times of the trucks on the static weight controlling systems. Some of the applications of such systems are legislation, regulations and administration of the transportation. Besides the cost of maintenance of the roads, such damages lead to environmental threats. WIM systems reduce the risk of accidents of over-weighted vehicles, reduce damages to the infrastructure such as roads or bridges and lead to time savings for both the truck drivers and for the police.

• Delivery space booking systems: By using such systems the space for parking could be booked for a specific vehicle at a specific time period to load or unload the freight. Such systems are quite useful in urban areas with space limitations like retailers placed in the large city centers. Also, they might be used for the terminals. These systems contribute to environmental and efficiency/effectiveness performance dimensions of the transportation operations by eliminating the non-value-adding time for searching for the parking space. The application of intelligent parking booking systems reduces the total number of vehicle trips during a specific time period (contributing to the environment) and maximizes the utilization of the parking place (contributing to the efficiency of transportation infrastructure).

• Vehicle location and condition monitoring systems: This system provides real-time information about the position of the vehicles on the map by transmitting the information via satellite. Such information is provided for the users via the web. By installing sensors on the vehicle, such as the container, the system can provide real-time information regarding the condition of the freights in shipment. It has the capability of real-time controlling if the container's door is locked or unlocked. It enables better fleet management and tracking and tracing of the goods and vehicles. For example, by having real-time information regarding the location of the trucks on the roads the customs service providers can identify the arrival time of the vehicles and prepare the documentation on the borders to decrease the waiting times of the trucks behind the borders. By using such information the port operators can send expected arrival time updates to the trucks in case of delays of the ships. Also, by having such a system the driver can find the safe or unsafe parking zones. It leads to an improvement of the security and safety of transportation. The supported dimensions of transportation after using such systems are effectiveness/efficiency and security/safety. The application of integrated vehicle tracking systems is useful as a part of decision support systems for transportation resource management and logistics management.

- Route planning systems: Such systems plan the route of transportation operations according to the situation of the roads. As a result, effectiveness of the operations is increased by providing a better level of service to the customers through reducing the delay potential. By reducing the waiting times on the roads the operations become more eco-friendly. Using such systems leads to better resource planning for the transportation operators. The dynamic vehicle routing and scheduling will be beneficial for carriers by reducing their costs, for customers by receiving a better level of service and for the environment by reducing the traffic congestion.

- Driving behavior monitoring and controlling systems: The speed and acceleration of the driver during the transportation operations is analyzed and feedback for improving the driving is given by using such systems. Such feedback leads to reducing the fuel consumption of the vehicles and therefore makes more eco-friendly transportation. Therefore, it supports the transportation resource management. Also, using technologies for controlling the concentration of the drivers during transportation leads to a reduction in accidents and to an improvement of the safety of operations.

- Crash preventing systems: Different technologies such as sensors are used on these systems to decrease the probability of accidents. For example, sensors installed on the car with the capability of sending signals to the driver when getting close to an object is one form of technology used on such systems. The other type of system has the capability to detect objects and provide information regarding the probability of accidents by measuring the distance from one vehicle to the other vehicles via the transportation infrastructure. In case of a pedestrian jumping in front of a vehicle a signal is sent to the other vehicle and leads to prevention of an accident. Such systems increase the safety of the transportation operations by reducing the probability of accidents. Systems for the detection of pedestrians at night are an example of this group.

- Freight location monitoring systems: The application of RFID tags without the need of direct light contact for scanning has created an advantage for the transportation operations. By installing the RFID readers on the vehicles or warehouse doors, the freight movement is automatically controlled and recorded in the information systems' databases. Using the auto-ID systems has provided new capabilities such as reading a large number of tags at the same time, and has decreased the amount of errors caused by manual data entry. Also, it has reduced inaccuracies about the number of items in inventories or in vehicles when warehousing or shipping. Using the auto-ID based tracking and tracing systems leads to ease in finding the items in the big warehouses, ports and terminals. Decreasing the loading and unloading time and more accuracy of the cargo information by such systems leads to better resource management. Such systems improve the safety and security of transported items by increasing visibility of freight location. For example, auto identification technologies can help to reduce the number of stolen items or it is used to distinguish the fake items from the original ones. Also, the usage of such systems for waste management contributes to having a better environment. The application of such systems for warehouse operations leads to improvement of working efficiency, reduction of operations cost, customer satisfaction enhancement and time savings in resource management activities.

• Freight status monitoring systems: The application of different sensors for measuring physical attributes of the goods such as their temperature, humidity, impact level, light level, and vibration level can create improvements in transportation operations. The application of such systems for controlling dangerous goods, medicines and fresh food is being increased. A combination of the sensors with auto identification technologies such as RFID provides new opportunities for better controlling and monitoring the flow of material through different actors in the supply chains. The application of RFID technology combined with sensors leads to more efficiency of the transportation operations. The usage of them for controlling the shipments of chemicals, explosives and other dangerous goods can lead to a more safe and eco-friendly transportation.

New Words and Expressions

commonality ['kɔmənəltɪ]	n. 公共,共性,平民
fruition [fruː'ɪʃ(ə)n]	n. 完成,成就;结果实
concurrent [kən'kʌrənt]	adj. 并发的;一致的;同时发生的
stakeholder ['steɪk.həʊldə(r)]	n. 利益相关者;赌金保管者
processable ['prəʊsesəbl]	adj. 可加工的;适合加工的
utilization [juːtəlaɪ'zeɪʃ(ə)n]	n. 利用,使用
transmission [trænz'mɪʃ(ə)n]	n. 传动装置,变速器,传递,传送,播送
	n. [数]共点,同时发生的事件
intermodal ['ɪntə.məʊdl]	adj. 联合运输的,用于综合运输的
proprietary [prə'praɪət(ə)ri]	n. 所有权,所有人
	adj. 所有的,专利,私人拥有的
Weigh-In-Motion (WIM)	行驶中称重
maintenance ['meɪntənəns]	n. 维护,维修,保持,生活费用
shipment ['ʃɪpmənt]	n. 装货;装载的货物
capability [.keɪpə'bɪlətɪ]	n. 可能,能力,容量
dynamic [daɪ'næmɪk]	adj. 动态的;动力的;动力学的;有活力的
	n. 动态;动力
feedback ['fiːdbæk]	n. 反馈;成果,资料;回复
consumption [kən'sʌmpʃ(ə)n]	n. 消费;消耗;肺痨
automatically [.ɔːtə'mætɪklɪ]	adv. 自动地;机械地;无意识地
warehousing ['weə(r).haʊzɪŋ]	n. (商业银行所提供的)周转性短期贷款储仓;
freight status monitoring systems	货运状态监测系统
vibration [vaɪ'breɪʃ(ə)n]	n. 振动;犹豫;心灵感应

Exercises

I. True or false

a) Due to the trend of nationalization and globalization in recent decades, the importance of logistics management has been growing in many kinds of areas.

b) Transportation occupies a quarter of the amount in the logistics costs and transportation systems influence the performance of logistics system hugely.

c) Integration for ITS and e-business alike is not a simple task, however, as it must engage with a large array of disparate entities covering technical and political areas.

d) Progress has been accomplished in introducing automation and advanced information and (some) decision technologies to freight terminals, port container terminals in particular.

e) By using delivery space booking systems the space for parking could be booked for a specific vehicle at a specific time period to load or unload the freight. Such systems are quite useful in suburban areas with space limitations like retailers placed in the large city centers.

II. Filling blanks

a) Materials management describes the movement of materials and components within a firm. Physical distribution _____ the movement of goods outward from the end of the assembly line to the customer.

b) The need to manage door-to-door deliveries efficiently on a global scale _____ the expansion of corporate information networks to include suppliers, dealers, partners, subsidiaries and alliances in an integrated manner.

c) One may argue, in fact, that the common ancestor to CVOS developments is the _____ by the freight-transportation industry of EDI, two-way communication, and vehicle (and cargo) location and tracking technologies.

d) This trend is actually _____ the electronic integration of carriers, operators of intermodal transfer facilities, and shippers with common interests in the movement of certain commodity groups or the utilization of particular infrastructures.

e) This system provides real-time information about the position of the vehicles on the map by _____ the information via satellite.

III. Translation

a) Transporting is required in the whole production procedures, from manufacturing to delivery to the final consumers and returns.

b) The application of information and communication technology (ICT) to transportation has also led to the emergence of Intelligent Transportation Systems (ITS).

c) Different technologies such as smart traffic lights, plate recognition cameras and speed measuring cameras equipped with sensors and variable traffic signs are used in such information systems.

6.2 Challenges of CVOS

6.2.1 Development of CVOS in Worldwide

The CVOS area of ITS has been defined as advanced systems aimed at simplifying and automating freight and fleet management operations at the institutional level.

National or regional authorities, in collaboration with carriers and firms that propose the required technologies, usually initiate CVOS projects. The goal is to increase the performance of the infrastructure (mostly highways) and customs systems, simplify and automate government control-related freight and fleet management operations, and, thus, enhance the efficiency of commercial vehicle activities through seamless operations based on electronic vehicle and cargo identification, location and tracking, pre-clearance and in-motion verifications. These systems rely heavily on vehicle or cargo positioning systems (GPS or radio frequency networks), bi-directional communications (DSRC - Dedicated Short Range Communications, radio, satellite, or wireless phone), and EDI. The importance of CVOS applications has been acknowledged quite early on in ITS history, and a significant number of CVOS projects have been undertaken or are currently under way.

Initial deployment efforts of CVOS technologies have been organized around the so-called "corridors". A corridor is typically organized around a major highway, or a system of highways, that cross several regional or national jurisdictions. The goal is to increase the fluidity of truck traffic and to offer seamless interstate or inter-nation border crossings, while ensuring adequate levels of control and reporting relative to regulations on safety, traffic, customs, and so on. Weight-in-motion scales, overweight detectors, EDI, automatic vehicle (and cargo) identification and classification systems, vision technology (to read license plates), and variable message signs are among the main technologies used. Corridor projects usually involve national and local governments and agencies, private technology providers (who, sometimes, also contribute significantly to the financing of the technology deployment), and, obviously, carriers.

Several corridor projects have been undertaken in the second half of the 1990s. In the United States, these efforts have led to the establishment of two major continental systems, the North American Preclearance and Safety System (NORPASS) and the PrePass Program. In July 2008, NORPASS included 11 members and partner states/provinces in the United States and Canada, while the PrePass network covered 49 states. In July 2008, some 425,000 trucks were enrolled with PrePass, which represents an almost 100% increase in 4 years. Both systems offer essentially the same services, weight station bypass (weight-in-motion when available) and are based on transponder technology. The technology now offers transponders that may be used with both systems. A carrier using such transponders and aiming to operate within both systems must register with each system separately, however, and pay the appropriate fees. Both systems offer compatibility with other transponder-based systems, e.g., electronic tolls and terminal access.

The TruckScan system installed in the state of New South Wales in Australia uses visual recognition systems coupled to electronic databases, in-motion screening testing for weight (per axle and overall), length and height, and vehicle guidance signs and tracking systems. This passive system is designed to automate and improve the roadside checking of vehicles. Various in-motion verification, monitoring, and pre-clearance systems are also deployed by Canadian Provinces.

In Japan, the emphasis is on the real-time collection of truck operational status and its distribution as basic data to operators, in line with the heavy promotion and use of advanced traveler information systems and in-vehicle navigation systems. Efforts are also directed toward the development of integrated and automated terminals, also called "logistic centers", new road management system with dedicated lines for freight vehicles, and an advanced road-vehicle communication and cruise-assist system.

In the European Community, the European Commission and the member states have embarked on a comprehensive effort of research, development, and deployment of ITS. It is an exemplary effort in its reach and scope, as well as in the framework it established for collaboration and partnership among all the stakeholders—government and public agencies, private firms, consulting bureaux, universities, research centers, and so on. The website of ERTICO together with those of its members details the many European projects. Two main directions are defined for Freight ITS in the policy of the European Commission. The first concerns the connection of the countries of Central and East Europe to the rest of the continent. ITS are seen as an essential tool to achieve this objective. The second direction concerns the development of intermodal transportation as the main mechanism to influence the current mode choice that is heavily biased toward trucks and highways. The document argues that the improvement of infrastructures, such as ports, and the enhancement of information and decision systems, will result in some of the cargo currently "on the road" to move to less environmentally invasive means of transportation such as rail and coastal and fluvial navigation.

6.2.2　Current Challenges of CVOS

A major class of CVOS projects, particularly widespread in North America, concerns border-crossing operations. This area has acquired a sense of urgency and high priority following the terrorist attacks on the United States and the continuing terrorist threat. Ports have thus become prime targets for ITS and e-business projects with security issues as the driving objective. While the urgency has been primarily felt in the United States, border CVOS are being developed worldwide. The main goal was and continues to be to clear drivers, vehicles, and cargo in order to speed up the passage of vehicles (trucks, containers, railcars) carrying manufactured and agricultural goods through the border inspection facilities, within the parameters set by the border control requirements in terms of security, immigration, illicit cargo, agricultural controls, etc.

The current state of the world affairs and the US response has elevated these issues at a level of urgency and complexity never felt before. The creation in the United States, in Canada, and elsewhere of new government structures dedicated to security issues including customs and border control illustrates this urgency.

Several security policies significantly increase delays at ports and border crossings and thus influence the efficiency of commerce and supply chains. Among others, the US Customs Container Security Initiative requires the inspection and pre-clearance of containers before they leave the port of origin or the last major transhipment port. The US Customs and Border Protection agency also requires advanced transmission of cargo information for shipments destined for the United States. Systems are being deployed to mitigate the associated significantly longer delays. For instance, US, Canadian, and Mexican customs commercial programs are being aligned (the Free and Secure Trade, FAST, program) to support moving preapproved goods quickly across borders. The program is based on registering and pre-approving import/export firms (shippers), carriers, and drivers.

For ports and border ITS/CVOS, as for most other ITS areas, the development of the "intelligence" part must accompany that of the hardware and the availability of information. Very few efforts have been undertaken in this area, however. The determination of the optimal number of containers to be inspected to satisfy the security requirements and to limit the delays in ports is an example of such a topic. Many challenges and opportunities are also offered by the intense automation of container terminals in ports.

6.2.3 CVISN for Safety Mission

The Federal Motor Carrier Safety Administration (FMCSA) was created as an operating administration within the U.S. Department of Transportation (USDOT) by the Motor Carrier Safety Improvement Act of 1999. The primary mission of the FMCSA is to reduce crashes, injuries, and fatalities involving large trucks and buses.

CVISN (pronounced "see-vision") stands for Commercial Vehicle Information Systems and Networks.

CVISN is a nationwide program managed by FMCSA rather an application. It supports safety mission by providing grant funds to States to:

- Improve safety and productivity of motor carriers, commercial vehicles and their drivers.
- Improve efficiency and effectiveness of commercial vehicle safety programs through targeted enforcement.
- Improve commercial vehicle data sharing within States and between States and FMCSA.
- Reduce Federal, State, and industry regulatory and administrative costs.

CVISN is a collection of information systems and communications networks that support CVOS. It is part of the larger ITS architecture and includes information systems owned and operated by governments, carriers, and other stakeholders. It excludes the sensor and control elements of CVOS.

CVISN consists of both Core and Expanded CVISN functionality. Core CVISN capabilities exist in three program areas:

Safety Information Exchange—designed to assure the safety of motor carriers and commercial vehicles through improved data collection and enhanced data sharing (e.g., inspection reports, credentials status) across agency and jurisdictional boundaries.

Specific Safety Information Exchange items include:

- Use the Aspen automated inspection software (an application, used by FMCSA and most State Commercial Motor Vehicle enforcement agencies, that collects all the commercial driver/vehicle roadside inspection details) at all major inspection sites.
- Connect to the national Safety and Fitness Electronic Records (SAFER) system to provide exchange of interstate carrier and vehicle safety data among States.
- Implement a State-specific Commercial Vehicle Information Exchange Window (CVIEW) system or an equivalent to exchange credential and safety data with the national SAFER system, which makes the data available to other jurisdictions.

Electronic Credentials Administration—designed to automate the application, processing, and issuance of motor carrier operating credentials and permits in order to improve the efficiency of both the motor carriers and the State credentialing agencies.

Specific Electronic Credentials Administration items include:

• Automate processing of International Registration Plan (IRP) and International Fuel Tax Agreement (IFTA) credentials and conduct at least 10 percent of transaction volume electronically.

• Participate in IRP Clearinghouse to share information across jurisdictions and automate funds settlement between jurisdictions.

• Participate in IFTA Clearinghouse to share information across jurisdictions and automate funds settlement between jurisdictions.

Electronic Screening—designed to target enforcement resources at high-risk and non- compliant motor carriers and commercial motor vehicles by identifying a commercial vehicle and verifying its safety and credentials information, as well as its weight, while it remains in motion. Vehicles known to be non-compliant or carriers with histories of poor safety performance are targeted for inspection while vehicles with the necessary operating credentials that are operated by a motor carrier with a history of good safety performance are allowed to bypass an inspection facility.

Specific Electronic Screening items include:

• Implement electronic screening at a minimum of one fixed or mobile inspection site, and be ready to replicate this functionality at other sites.

Once a State is certified as having deployed all of the Core CVISN functionality, it is deemed to be Core CVISN Compliant and must maintain these capabilities. Once Core CVISN Compliant, a State may use its Federal CVISN Deployment Grant funding to deploy Expanded CVISN functionality. The Expanded portion of the CVISN program is designed to be more flexible than the Core component of the program.

States are not required to deploy a set of fixed capabilities or to enable certain technologies as part of expanded CVISN but rather are able to choose the capabilities that they wish to deploy. This "cafeteria approach" allows States to customize their Expanded CVISN programs and focus their technology resources on the projects that are most important to their needs.

While States can deploy a wide variety of capabilities as part of their Expanded CVISN programs, the FMCSA supports a set of key capabilities. The FMCSA, in conjunction with public and private stakeholders, initially identified 40 capabilities that could be integrated into the CVISN program. These capabilities were segmented into four Expanded CVISN program areas:

• Driver Information Sharing;
• Enhanced Safety Information Sharing;
• Smart Roadside;
• Expanded Electronic Credentialing.

By August 2012, 29 States had deployed all aspects of Core CVISN and were certified as Core CVISN Compliant. All States and the District of Columbia have deployed at least one element of Core CVISN functionality and many States are close to achieving Core CVISN Compliance. The CVISN deployment phase for all states and DC is shown in Figure 6.1.

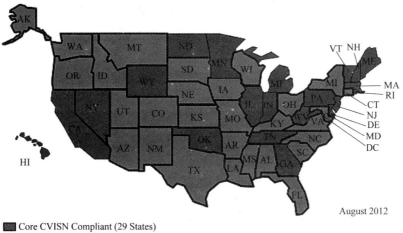

Figure 6.1 Deployment of core CVISN functionality as of August 2012

New Words and Expressions

collaboration with	与……合作
rely on, rely upon	依赖于
jurisdiction[ˌdʒʊərɪsˈdɪkʃ(ə)n]	n. 司法权,裁判权
fluidity[fluˈɪdətɪ]	n. 流动性
interstate[ˌɪntə(r)ˈsteɪt]	n. 洲际
corridor[ˈkɑrɪdɔː(r)]	n. 走廊
continental[ˌkɑntɪˈnent(ə)l]	n. 大陆
enrolled with	登记
bypass[ˈbaɪˌpɑːs]	n. 旁路
verification[ˌverɪfɪˈkeɪʃ(ə)n]	n. 验证
commission[kəˈmɪʃ(ə)n]	n. 委员会,委员
intermodal[ˈɪntəˌməʊdl]	n. 联运
invasive[ɪnˈveɪsɪv]	adj. 侵入的
fluvial[ˈfluːvɪəl]	n. 河流
illicit[ɪˈlɪsɪt]	adj. 非法的
dedicate to	献给
align[əˈlaɪn]	v. 对齐
register[ˈredʒɪstə(r)]	v. 注册
fatality[fəˈtælətɪ]	n. 死亡
stakeholder[ˈsteɪk.həʊldə(r)]	n. 利益相关者
jurisdictional[dʒʊrɪsˈdɪkʃənl]	adj. 管辖权的
implement[ˈɪmpləmənt]	vt. 实施,执行;使生效,实现
equivalent[ɪˈkwɪvələnt]	adj. 相当的,等效的
participate in	分担,参与
credential[krəˈdenʃl]	n. 证书,执照,国书,信任状

target for	针对
portion of	部分
integrate into	融入

Exercises

I. True or false

a) By August 2013, 29 States had deployed all aspects of Core CVISN and were certified as Core CVISN Compliant.

b) In Japan, the emphasis is on the real-time collection of truck operational status and its distribution as basic data to operators, in line with the heavy promotion and use of advanced traveler information systems and in-vehicle navigation systems.

c) The Federal Motor Carrier Safety Administration (FMCSA) was created as an operating administration within the U. S. Department of Transportation (USDOT) by the Motor Carrier Safety Improvement Act of 1999.

d) The Expanded portion of the CVISN program is designed to be less flexible than the core component of the program.

e) For ports and border ITS/CVOS, as for most other ITS areas, the development of the "intelligence" part must accompany that of the hardware and the availability of information.

II. Filling blanks

a) Initial deployment efforts of CVOS technologies have been _____ around the so-called "corridors".

b) In July 2008, some 425,000 trucks were _____ with PrePass, which represents an almost 100% increase in 4 years.

c) Several security policies _____ increase delays at ports and border crossings and thus influence the efficiency of commerce and supply chains.

d) It is part of the larger ITS architecture and _____ information systems owned and operated by governments, carriers, and other stakeholders.

e) Once a State is _____ as having deployed all of the Core CVISN functionality, it is deemed to be Core CVISN Compliant and must maintain these capabilities.

III. Translation

a) A corridor is typically organized around a major highway, or a system of highways, that cross several regional or national jurisdictions.

b) The Federal Motor Carrier Safety Administration (FMCSA) was created as an operating administration within the U. S. Department of Transportation (USDOT) by the Motor Carrier Safety Improvement Act of 1999.

c) It is part of the larger ITS architecture and includes information systems owned and operated by governments, carriers, and other stakeholders.

6.3 Electronic Screening System for the State of Missouri

The State of Missouri is actively pursuing a project that will allow commercial vehicles to have electronic screening service available at the weigh/inspection stations along major highways throughout the state with the application of currently available Intelligent Transportation Systems (ITS) technologies. With this electronic screening concept, vehicles that are safe and legal and have no outstanding out-of-service citations will be able to pass the weigh/inspection facility without delay. The Missouri ITS/Commercial Vehicle Operations (CVO) project proposes to combine technologies currently used in electronic toll collection (ETC) with a fiber optic communication system available along 350 miles of interstate highway in Missouri.

Commercial vehicles traveling the Oklahoma and Kansas Turnpikes often travel through Missouri as well, and both turnpike authorities have adopted Electronic Toll and Traffic Management (ETTM) processes and technologies that include the use of Automatic Vehicle Identification (AVI) transponders (tags) to pass through toll facilities without delay. This provides an opportunity to bundle ITS/CVO services with ITS/ETC services in compatible vehicle-to-roadside communication systems.

This article presents the following information: existing conditions for commercial vehicle operations and the communicationsinfrastructure in Missouri; a discussion of tag technologies; architecture of the proposed Missouri Electronic Screening System; and current status of planning and implementation.

6.3.1 Introduction

State agencies in Missouri are interested in the application of intelligent transportation systems technologies to improve the efficiency and safety of commercial vehicle operations (CVO). The CVO vision shared by state agencies in Missouri is the same as the National Intelligent Transportation Systems (ITS) Program Plan developed by ITS America for the Federal Highway Administration (FHWA). The vision is assisted by advanced technology, trucks and buses will move safely and freely throughout North America. The applied technology will take the form of electronic screening that will enable transponder-equipped trucks and buses to have safety status, credentials, and weight checked at mainline speeds. Vehicles that are safe and legal and have no outstanding out-of-service citations will usually be allowed to pass the weigh/inspection facility without delay.

The Missouri Department of Transportation (MoDOT) and the Missouri State Highway Patrol (MSHP) have jointly undertaken a number of initiatives to promote the economic well-being of Missouri and the nation by facilitating goods movement for business, industry, and motor carriers. In addition to the Kansas-Missouri ITS Institutional Issues Study conducted at the request of MoDOT, Missouri has developed an ITS/CVO Standing Committee at the state level including all agencies contributing to commercial vehicle operations. The ITS/CVO Standing Committee is charged with implementation of the Memorandum of Agreement (MOA) for ITS/CVO that has been signed by the directors of the following organizations:

1) MoDOT;
2) MSHP;
3) Missouri Department of Revenue (MDOR);

4) Missouri Department of Economic Development;

5) Missouri Division Office of the FHWA;

6) Office of Motor Carriers of the FHWA;

7) Missouri Motor Carriers Association.

This MOA has also been signed by the governor of the state of Missouri.

Missouri has also been successful in obtaining participation from the private sector for support of ITS/CVO programs. In cooperation with MoDOT, a private company has laid several hundred miles of fiber optic cable in the highway rights of way throughout the state. MoDOT and MSHP have participated in the design and installation of the network to provide for nodes at weigh stations throughout the state. Once completed, the entire communications infrastructure will be in place with the capability to link the MSHP's mainframe computers to the fixed weigh stations. The fiber optic network will provide the avenue required to process data transmission at the speeds necessary for electronic clearance of commercial vehicles traveling at mainline highway speeds.

6.3.2 Existing Conditions

Primary responsibility for motor carrier regulation and credentialing is shared by four agencies in the Missouri:

1) MoDOT;

2) MDOR;

3) Missouri Department of Economic Development, Division of Motor Carrier and Railroad Safety (MCRS);

4) MSHP.

MoDOT administers the oversize/overweight (OS/OW) permit program in the state of Missouri. Carriers wishing to operate a vehicle that exceeds Missouri dimensional or weight limits must obtain an OS/OW permit for that vehicle. Carriers moving loads exceeding 120,000 pounds Gross Vehicle Weight (GVW) may be subject to bridge stress studies, which are conducted by the DOT.

The MDOR oversees several motor carrier functions including vehicle titling and registration (including the International Registration Plan, or IRP, for interstate carriers); motor fuel taxes (International Fuel Tax Agreement or IFTA); commercial drivers licensing; and the issuance of temporary permits. In conjunction with these functions, the MDOR is responsible for accepting and reviewing applications, issuing credentials to approved carriers, and auditing and collecting fees when required.

The MCRS Division in the Department of Economic Development is responsible for regulating common, contract, and private motor carriers in the state of Missouri. Motor carriers that fall into one of these categories and conduct intrastate or interstate operation must obtain operating authority from the MCRS. MCRS operating authority may be granted to motor carriers who are registered with the Interstate Commerce Commission (ICC), as well as to ICC-exempt carriers.

The MSHP enforces the credentials issued by the agencies listed above and operates all fixed and mobile enforcement facilities. The MSHP is also responsible for administration of the Motor

Carrier Safety Assistance Program (MCSAP) funded by FHWA. Weight and safety enforcement is the responsibility of the MSHP's Commercial Vehicle Enforcement (CVE) Unit. Vehicles may be weighed at fixed inspection stations located throughout the state or by mobile inspection units. The CVE Unit also conducts vehicle and driver inspections. Enforcement personnel have the authority to put drivers out of service for certain vehicle or driver safety violations, or for operating without the proper credentials.

Under the current weight enforcement strategy, all trucks must stop at weigh stations when the scales are open. This causes unnecessary delays for legal carriers, and the requirement for all of the trucks to exit and enter the traffic flow may have a negative impact on safety. Under the current enforcement system, driver and vehicle credentials cannot be inspected without the truck stopping, either at a weigh station or a roadside spot check. Requiring all trucks to stop, whether or not they are operating legally, dilutes the effectiveness of enforcement efforts and reduces carrier productivity.

The State of Missouri currently operates weigh stations at 19 locations. During 1995, the Center for Transportation Research and Education (CTRE) conducted a study for Missouri to focus on the enforcement activities that currently take place at the permanent weigh stations and to investigate Automatic Vehicle Identification (AVI) technologies that could be easily implemented for electronic screening at the weigh stations along I-70 and I-44, the two interstate highways through Missouri.

By the studying of general traffic flow information at the two weigh stations, it is known that I-70 carries the highest volume of truck traffic with more than 7,500 trucks using this route each day, and I-44 is the second busiest with truck volumes over 6,000 per day.

A communications infrastructure is also in place that can serve the weigh stations along I-44 and I-70. The extent of the fiber optic network for ITS communications has been developed along highway rights of way throughout Missouri. The fiber optic network will provide the avenue required to process data transmission at the speeds necessary for electronic screening of commercial vehicles traveling at mainline highway speeds. The fixed weigh stations along I-44 and I-70 will be able to communicate with the mainframe computers of the Highway Patrol located in Jefferson City.

The Oklahoma and Kansas Turnpikes have adopted Electronic Toll and Traffic Management (ETTM) processes and technology that include the use of AVI transponders (tags) to pass through toll facilities without delay. Trucks operating on I-44 and I-70 in Missouri are often users of the Oklahoma and Kansas Turnpikes and may already have toll tags on the vehicles. Both turnpike authorities have selected a common technology so future customers will not have to purchase more than one tag and to assure compatibility between the toll facilities.

MoDOT decided to investigate the use of enhanced toll tags to facilitate electronic screening for trucks at weigh stations on I-44 and I-70. Because trucks operating on the Oklahoma and Kansas Turnpikes are likely to already have toll tags, the same identification tags could be used to identify trucks with valid and current Commercial Vehicle Safety Alliance (CVSA) safety inspections and with current and valid credentials. In conjunction with mainline Weigh-In-Motion (WIM), the opportunity appears to exist, at a minimum level of investment and risk (both financial and technical), to electronically screen trucks for current safety inspections and possibly for credentials and weight.

As a first step in determining if those toll collection transponders currently on commercial vehicles could support electronic screening at weigh stations, MoDOT first wished to know approximately how many tag-equipped trucks were currently passing the weigh stations. Field data were collected during the summer of 1995 in order to estimate the number of trucks passing weigh stations along I-44 and I-70 that are currently equipped with toll tags from either Oklahoma or Kansas.

During June 1995, an AVI reader system was placed along the side of the eastbound travel lanes of I-44 just before the exit ramp for the Joplin weigh station. Data were recorded from Monday, June 12, 1995 through Tuesday, June 20, 1995, and the highest number of tags recorded was more than 1,500 on Friday, June 16, 1995. The vehicles carrying tags from the Oklahoma Turnpike Authority (OTA) were easily identifiable in the tag numbers recorded, and the OTA tags ranged from 89 percent to 94 percent of the total number of tags recorded.

During the time period that the toll tags were recorded, traffic volumes from a nearby permanent count station showed eastbound travel on I-44 at approximately 8,000 vehicles on weekdays (range = 7,378 vehicles per day to 8,571 vehicles per day). Total traffic on Friday, Saturday and Sunday was substantially higher with volumes ranging from about 10,000 vehicles per day to more than 11,000. The percent of vehicles in the eastbound traffic flow with toll tags ranged from about 24 percent to 35 percent.

The AVI reader system was also placed along the eastbound travel lanes of Interstate 70 at the Odessa weigh station from June 22 through July 10, 1995. The data records of the tag readings were not useable for the entire time period, but for the days with valid data, the number of toll tags recorded on I-70 ranged from 215 to 513 per day.

The number of vehicles equipped with toll tags is currently much higher along I-44 (with a maximum reading of more than 1,500) than along I-70 (with a maximum reading of slightly over 500). Vehicles from the Oklahoma Turnpike are not as likely to be traveling on I-70 since there is no direct connection from Oklahoma. Vehicles from the Kansas Turnpike are much more likely to be traveling on I-70, but the Kansas Turnpike Authority only began using ETTM during 1995 and penetration of the toll tags has not reached the level that is seen in Oklahoma. (The OTA has been using electronic toll payment since 1991). In general, the information collected about current toll tag use along I-44 and I-70 shows that a sufficient number of vehicles are currently equipped with tags to support building on this technology for CVO electronic screening.

6.3.3 Compatibility of Transponder (TAG) Technologies

The Oklahoma and Kansas Turnpikes have adopted ETTM processes and technologies that include the use of AVI transponders (tags) to pass through toll facilities without delay. Common to all Electronic Toll Collection (ETC) systems are a vehicle-mounted transponder/tag, a reading device, and a computer system for processing and storing data.

AVI or tag technologies and systems are often categorized as being either "Read Only" or

"Read/Write". ETTM and CVO use the same terms to describe tag functionality. The three types of tags commonly envisioned to support electronic screening and ETTM applications are:

- Type I -Supports only one-way transmission of an identifier or other fixed information from the transponder to the roadside reader.
- Type II -Supports two-way data transmissions and, typically, a variable message component. This allows the transmission of variable data to the transponder at one reader (such as location identification and time stamp), and the subsequent transmission of that data from the tag to another reader.
- Type III -Supports not only two-way transmission of data, but also supports electronic communication interfaces to external devices mounted on the vehicle, such as onboard computers. This allows data to be sent from an onboard computer to the tag, and from there transmitted to a roadside reader. Similarly, information from a roadside reader can be transmitted to the transponder and from there sent to an onboard computer or signaling device to be read by the truck driver.

The technological basis for transponder technology is not new. Its origins can be traced to the use of Identification Friend or Foe (IFF) interrogation employed during World War II. Aircraft detected by radar could not be readily identified as friendly; radio contact with the pilot could confirm the nature of the aircraft. However, in the absence of direct pilot confirmation, "friendly" could not be established. This problem was solved by placing a transponder in the friendly aircraft. As the aircraft entered radar range, the transponder was interrogated and a code was exchanged between the aircraft and security establishing the aircraft as friendly.

From that early beginning, tags can now be used to support electronic screening. The basic differences among various tag technologies lie in the communications medium, the sophistication of the communications protocol between tag and reader, and the extent of tag "intelligence". The majority of systems currently utilize some form of radio frequency identification (RFID) scheme to establish reliable communications between tag and reader. The carrier frequency of choice lies in the 902 - 928 MHz band, but others operate as high as 2450 MHz (2.45 GHz) and as low as 134 kHz. Radio Frequency (RF) tags can be further differentiated by whether they merely modulate the carrier signal (passive or backscatter tag) transmitted by the reader and reflect the signal back to the reader or contain an internal transmitter (active tag), capable of replying when the reader is not transmitting.

The Pike Pass tags of the OTA are Type I, and the Kansas tags are Type II. Both turnpike authorities have selected a common technology, backscatter, with the tags manufactured by Amtech.

Most major toll agencies in the United States either have Dedicated Short Range Communications (DSRC) systems in current revenue service or have made the decision to install DSRC and have selected a technical solution. By the end of 1994, approximately 500,000 tags were in use, by 1995 this number had doubled to 1 million, and by the end of 1996 it doubled again to 2 million. CVO applications currently include approximately 10,000 users on the two major CVO applications (HELP Inc. and Advantage I-75) as well as several border crossing projects on the borders of Texas, California, New York and Michigan.

The OTA began using electronic toll payment in 1991, and a 1996 survey by International Bridge, Tunnel and Turnpike Association (IBTTA) showed that the OTA had the largest number of ETC customer accounts. Based on March 1997 information provided by Amtech (letter dated 3/10/97), the OTA has approximately 332,000 customer accounts for ETC tags, of which about 75,000 are issued to accounts for commercial vehicles of a classification that would have to stop at weigh stations. The Kansas Turnpike Authority began ETC operations in late 1995 and currently has 65,000 customer accounts for toll tags. Fifty thousand of these Kansas accounts are for commercial accounts such as trucking or other service businesses. The Amtech tags used by Oklahoma and Kansas currently amount to almost 400,000 of the estimated 2 million customer accounts (about 20 percent) that are in place nationwide for ETC operations.

Tag technologies have evolved, and continue to evolve, on the basis of technological advancements and market requirements. Various standards setting activities are currently underway, and Missouri plans to evaluate both the existing RFID population and other tag technologies as the state moves forward with implementation of electronic screening.

6.3.4 Proposed Architecture

The term "architecture" is used in many contexts with varying definitions. For research currently being conducted for ITS, the overall structure (i.e., major components and interfaces) and unifying design characteristics (i.e., principles and standards) of a system are referred to as the architecture of that system. This section will describe a general architecture for electronic screening for the state of Missouri. The architecture is intended to provide guidance to implementers of the CVO electronic screening system.

The MSHP currently verifies the following information when trucks come through the weigh stations:

(1) Vehicles are weighed to check for compliance with weight limits, and if overweight, the vehicle is checked for a valid OW permit from MoDOT;

(2) Vehicle credentials may be checked to verify that the vehicle has all necessary permits to operate in the state of Missouri;

(3) Vehicle credentials may be checked to verify that the vehicle has paid fuel tax and has a fuel permit;

(4) Driver credentials may be checked to verify that the driver has a valid Commercial Driver's License (CDL) to operate a commercial vehicle in the State of Missouri;

(5) Vehicle inspection may occur to determine if the vehicle meets all applicable vehicle safety codes.

Under the current weight enforcement procedures, all trucks must stop at weigh stations in Missouri when the scales are open. The credentials of trucks and drivers cannot be inspected without the truck stopping, either at a weigh station or a roadside spot check.

Through the WIM scale and AVI reader, many credential checks and inspection actions could be accomplished by verification of information on a transponder or by automated field review.

In order to accomplish the screening actions, information exchange will need to be accomplished very effectively. Information exchange will be required between the following state government agencies involved in motor carrier functions: MDOR, MoDOT, and MSHP.

For the general architecture of the proposed Missouri Electronic Screening System and identifies subsystems that Missouri can evaluate for implementation, it is organized beginning at the Roadway AVI and WIM subsystem and flowing to the subsystem of the processors at the weigh stations. The weigh station processors then connect to the processors at the state, regional and national levels.

6.3.5 Alternatives for Implementation

Missouri will consider two alternatives to support implementation of the Roadway AVI and WIM subsystem for electronic screening:

(1) Missouri owning the Roadway AVI and WIM subsystem;

(2) Missouri contracting with a company to provide the data necessary to support the Roadway AVI and WIM subsystem for electronic screening.

Although many options could be considered for this subsystem of electronic screening, ownership and contracting are the two major alternatives. Other options could include contracting for only certain elements of the Roadway AVI and WIM subsystem, such as training or maintenance.

If Missouri decides to pursue ownership of the Roadway AVI and WIM subsystem, this will include purchasing the equipment, either installing or contracting the installation, commissioning the subsystem, and maintaining the subsystem. Contracting for the service will include the establishment of an agreement with a company to provide the data necessary to support roadside electronic screening. In either case, Missouri will make a financial and technical resource investment.

A first step toward conducting a financial analysis which will support the decision that Missouri either own the subsystem or contract for data, is identifying the associated cost elements. The Cost Elements are subdivided into non-recurring and recurring. Non-recurring costs are typically incurred once during the program, and periodic charges are incurred for recurring costs. Each of the cost elements is discussed in the following paragraphs.

The non-recurring costs include the following elements:

- Equipment costs will include transponders, AVI readers, WIM, computer processors associated with AVI/WIM located in the weigh station, traffic control in the weigh station and support cable. Support cable includes interconnecting cable, junction boxes and termination points.
- Software includes all AVI and WIM operational software, software interfacing the AVI and WIM, weigh station computer software associated with the site and software interfaces with databases off the site.
- Installation costs include all mounting, trenching, and placement of equipment and support cable. For the WIM installation, ASTM E 1318-94, "Standard Specification for Highway Weigh-in-Motion (WIM) Systems with User Requirements and Test Method", provides guidance.
- A subsystem test includes testing the AVI, WIM, weigh station processors, and communications with off-site databases. More specifically, AVI tests include antenna placement and field test readings and interface with WIM. WIM testing includes a calibration of the equipment accord-

ing to ASTM standard E1318-94, Standard Specification for Highway Weigh-in-Motion (WIM) Systems with User Requirements and Test Method. The weigh station computer is tested to insure truck information, traffic control, and communications with off-site databases are functioning correctly.

• Subsystem commissioning follows testing and brings the subsystem to an operational condition.

• Training enforcement staff to operate the electronic screening system includes fully familiarizing officers with the roadside subsystem technology and function in addition to the functionality of the weigh station computer screens, outputs, and weigh station traffic control system. Training technical staff to perform both preventive and corrective maintenance includes a detailed course in both the subsystem and site element and logical troubleshooting techniques.

• AVI and WIM site rehabilitation depends on the site condition. ASTM 1318-94 can be used as a standard to describe the preferred site condition and expected WIM performance level.

The recurring costs include the following elements:

• Outside services can include such things as telecommunication charges when communication with remote databases may require using a commercially available network that charges a rate per minute of usage.

• The technical staff and support for subsystem maintenance will include all personnel and the support services needed for maintaining the Roadway AVI and WIM. Technical staff includes engineers and technicians located at a central location and at field locations. Technical staff will require support to include test equipment, repair parts, and a vehicle to travel among sites. For example, test equipment will include not only instrumentation necessary to troubleshoot the AVI, WIM and interconnecting cable; it may include a cell phone to transmit equipment characteristics to a central location for further analysis.

• Preventive maintenance includes AVI, WIM, and site checks to make sure the equipment is operating within specifications and the site is in an acceptable condition. Data generated by the AVI and WIM and stored in the weigh station computer can be analyzed to identify drift that could lead to deterioration of the AVI and WIM performance levels. Depending on the condition of the site, an inspection of the WIM should be conducted at least once a year to spot pavement deterioration that will cause site performance to drift outside specification.

• Corrective maintenance is a result of equipment or site failure. For example, a lightning strike can cause the equipment to malfunction. Site failures can occur due to an unexpected pavement breakup. The frequency of corrective maintenance is impossible to predict, but will require immediate action by maintenance staff.

• Subsystem upgrades can be a function of both subsystemobsolescence and a desire to increase subsystem performance levels. Subsystem obsolescence occurs due to improvements in technology. For example, as transponder technology continues to improve and migrate toward evolving markets and standards, it may become necessary to consider redesigning the site or buying new readers, processors and software.

• Periodic contract charges apply specifically to charges that result from ownership of the subsystem resting with a service provider and not Missouri. The periodic contract charges replace major cost elements in both non-recurring and recurring categories.

If Missouri decides to pursue a contract agreement with a service provider, this will relieve Missouri of the responsibility for major non-recurring and recurring tasks. However, establishing a contract with a service provider will require that Missouri conduct a very focused effort in contract administration. For example, the contract must clearly establish the time period for the service provider to replace failed equipment and to have malfunctioning software back in operation. Further, the Missouri contract administrator must make sure the service provider meets the downtime specification in the agreement. Therefore, although Missouri will be relieved of subsystem facility maintenance and upgrading, Missouri's contract administrator must assertively follow up on service provider performance levels established in the contract agreement.

During the coming year, the State of Missouri will be actively working on implementation of a CVO Electronic Screening System that builds on toll tag technology. This will include a bid process that will allow the state to perform financial evaluation of ownership versus contracting for service.

New Words and Expressions

electronic screening	电子筛查
out-of-service	报废
fiber optic communication system	光纤通信
turnpike ['tɜː(r)nˌpaɪk]	n. 付费公路,收费关卡
Automatic Vehicle Identification (AVI)	自动车辆识别
implementation [ˌɪmplɪmən'teɪʃ(ə)n]	n. 实现
Federal Highway Administration (FHWA)	联邦高速公路管理局
Missouri Motor Carriers Association	密苏里州电机运营商协会
in conjunction with	连同;共同;与……协力
Interstate Commerce Commission (ICC)	州际商务委员会
enforcement facilities	执法机构
dilute [daɪ'luːt-'ljuːt]	vt. 稀释,冲淡,淡化
eastbound ['iːs(t)ˌbaʊnd]	adj. 东行的,向东的
penetration [ˌpenə'treɪʃ(ə)n]	n. 渗透;突破;侵入;洞察力
vehicle-mounted	车载;装在车上的
envision [ɪn'vɪʒ(ə)n]	vt. 想象,展望
Identification Friend or Foe (IFF)	敌我识别,二次雷达
interrogation [ɪnˌterə'geɪʃ(ə)n]	n. 询问,审问
radio frequency identification (RFID)	无线射频识别
modulate ['mɔdjʊleɪt]	vt. 调整,调制,调节
transmitter [trænz'mɪtə]	n. 发射机;传达人
Dedicated Short Range Communications (DSRC)	专用短程通信
estimate ['estɪmeɪt]	n. 估计;预计;估算

establishment [ɪˈstæblɪʃmənt]　　　　　　n. 建立, 确立
periodic [ˌpɪəriˈɔdɪk]　　　　　　　　　adj. 周期的
American Society of Testing Materials (ASTM)　美国材料实验协会
antenna placement　　　　　　　　　　天线位置
calibration [ˌkæləˈbreɪʃ(ə)n]　　　　　　n. 校准
corrective maintenance　　　　　　　　设备维护
obsolescence [ˌɔbsəˈles(ə)ns]　　　　　　n. 障碍

Exercises

I. True or false

a) The applied technology will take the form of electronic screening that will enable transponder-equipped trucks and buses to have safety status, credentials, and weight checked at mainline speeds.

b) The fiber optic network will provide the avenue required to process data transmission at the speeds necessary for electronic clearance of commercial vehicles traveling at mainline highway speeds.

c) In the state of Missouri, carriers wishing to operate a vehicle that exceeds Missouri dimensional or weight limits must obtain an OS/OW permit for that vehicle issued by the MSHP.

d) The MCRS Division in the Department of Economic Development is responsible for regulating common, contract, and private motor carriers in the state of Missouri.

e) Enforcement personnel in the MoDOT have the authority to put drivers out of service for certain vehicle or driver safety violations, or for operating without the proper credentials.

II. Filling blanks

a) With this electronic screening concept, vehicles that are safe and legal and have no outstanding out-of-service citations will be allowed to pass the weigh/inspection facility _____ delay.

b) In cooperation _____ MoDOT, a private company has laid several hundred miles of fiber optic cable in the highway rights of way throughout the state.

c) In conjunction with these functions, the MDOR is _____ for accepting and reviewing applications, issuing credentials to approved carriers, and auditing and collecting fees when required.

d) Automatic Vehicle Identification (AVI) or tag technologies and systems are often categorized as being _____ "Read Only" or "Read/Write".

e) Equipment costs will include transponders, AVI readers, WIM, computer processors associated _____ AVI/WIM located in the weigh station, traffic control in the weigh station and support cable. Support cable includes interconnecting cable, junction boxes and termination points.

III. Translation

a) This article presents the following information: existing conditions for commercial vehicle operations and the communications infrastructure in Missouri; a discussion of tag technologies; architecture of the proposed Missouri Electronic Screening System; and current status of planning and implementation.

b) Missouri has developed an ITS/CVO Standing Committee at the state level including all agencies contributing to commercial vehicle operations. The ITS/CVO Standing Committee is charged with implementation of the Memorandum of Agreement (MOA) for ITS/CVO that has been signed by the directors of the following organizations:

(1) Missouri Department of Transportation (MoDOT);

(2) Missouri State Highway Patrol (MSHP);

(3) Missouri Department of Revenue (MDOR);

(4) Missouri Department of Economic Development;

(5) Missouri Division Office of the Federal Highway Administration (FHWA);

(6) Office of Motor Carriers of the FHWA;

(7) Missouri Motor Carriers Association.

This MOA has also been signed by the governor of the state of Missouri.

c) Under the current weight enforcement strategy, all trucks must stop at weigh stations when the scales are open. This causes unnecessary delays for legal carriers, and the requirement for all of the trucks to exit and enter the traffic flow may have a negative impact on safety. Under the current enforcement system, driver and vehicle credentials cannot be inspected without the truck stopping, either at a weigh station or a roadside spot check. Requiring all trucks to stop, whether or not they are operating legally, dilutes the effectiveness of enforcement efforts and reduces carrier productivity.

Key to Exercises

Chapter 1　Intelligent Transportation Systems(ITS)

1.1　The Evolution of Transport

Ⅰ. True or false
a)T
b)T
c)F
d)F
e)T

Ⅱ. Choosing the best answer
a)C
b)D
c)D
d)B
e)D

Ⅲ. Translation
　　a)我们的目的是从针对交通运输系统的分析中得到一些结论,从而使我们能够在理解过去旅行行为的同时为将来的旅行做准备。
　　b)1800年,由罗马人兴建的大型道路网络,至今仍然为欧洲大部分国家承担政府行政信使服务以及运送军队和物资的工作。
　　c)在世界上可供选择的10亿辆车中,给车辆提供动力的大电池由在回收和处理方面都存在着大问题的有毒金属(如铅和镉)制造。

1.2　Introduction to ITS

Ⅰ. True or false
a)T
b)F
c)F
d)T

e) T

II. Filling blanks

a) integrating

b) of

c) deal

d) to

e) who

III. Translation

a) 不过,诸如交通事故、交通拥堵、环境污染、燃料的大量消耗等多方面的问题成为全人类所要面对的棘手问题,解决这些问题需要我们有根本的解决方案。

b) 智能交通系统提供了解决的思路和途径。在不久的将来,智能交通系统就能够在安全性、舒缓拥堵、驾驶舒适性和环境友好方面实现重大的技术突破,从而提供较当前道路交通系统所能提供的更为高层次的服务。

c) ITS,也就是智能交通(或运输)系统,提供了解决的思路和途径。ITS 技术使我们在建造更加智能化的基础设施以满足将来需要的同时也能够更好地利用当前已有的交通网络。更为重要的是,ITS 技术的实施可以帮助我们拯救生命,节约时间和金钱,以及保护环境。

1.3 Call for Papers IEEE-ITSC2013

I. True or false

a) T

b) T

c) F

d) F

e) F

II. Filling blanks

a) in the field

b) attending

c) annual

d) Selected

e) subject

III. Translation

a) 只要你在智能交通系统中从事研究、开发、设计、实施、规划和决策的工作,只要你属于科研院所、交通工业、汽车制造和供应厂商、政府、区域交通机构、国家实验室、国际组织、公交机构、货物运输机构、公交运输机构、服务提供商、电信机构、系统集成机构、商船运输、道路机构、车辆管理机构以及所有其他在能源和环境领域对交通系统有兴趣的机构,只要你参加这个独特的会议就会有所收益。

b) IEEE-ITSC2013 的会议主题是为所有交通模式服务的智能交通系统。信息和通信科技方面的主要进步在交通领域正在造就大量的可能。

c) 以 PDF 格式完成的初稿必须通过电子格式提交以便进行符合 IEEE 标准的同行评议。在会议网站即可找到详细的提交指引。

Chapter 2 Advanced Transportation Management Systems (ATMS)

2.1 Sensing Traffic Using Sensors

Ⅰ. True or false

a) T
b) F
c) F
d) T
e) F

Ⅱ. Filling blanks

a) between
b) Determine
c) decrease
d) reduces
e) determine

Ⅲ. Translation

a) 有许多技术方法可用来检测车辆,范围从超声波检测到环形线圈感应。在交通管制和控制中,环形线圈技术无疑是最可靠的。

b) 检测失误可以归咎于两个因素。首先,最明显的原因是,车身较高的表面覆盖金属的车辆离环形线圈较远,这会使车辆检测更加困难。其次,不太明显的原因是较大车辆的转弯半径也较大。

c) 作为一个系统,环形线圈感应是相对简单的,但重要的是通过了解它如何工作以及如何相互影响的相关知识将自己武装起来。毫无疑问,安装过程中充满问题会非常令人沮丧,但如果你将其分解为一个又一个的基本问题就可以更有效地解决这些问题。

2.2 Traffic Surveillance and Management

Ⅰ. True or false

a) T
b) F
c) F
d) T
e) T

Ⅱ. Filling blanks

a) utilized
b) necessary
c) staggering
d) regulated
e) provide

Ⅲ. Translation

a) 交通管制是一种不论夜间或白天都长时间在各种天气状况下工作的户外职业,而且由于可能受到来往车辆的碰撞而被认为是一个高风险的危险职业。

b) 交通管制人员可能仅是一个人对一个死胡同进行简单的改道或关闭运行控制,也可能多到由两至三人为一组共同处理某个复杂的任务。

c) 在加拿大新斯科舍,培训是由新斯科舍的交通和基础设施更新部负责管理,可为交通控制人员提供一天的课程学习,为临时地点的信号设置人员提供为期两天的课程。

2.3 Electronic Toll Collection (ETC)

Ⅰ. True or false

a) T

b) F

c) F

d) T

e) T

Ⅱ. Filling blanks

a) without

b) created

c) through

d) distinguish

e) before

Ⅲ. Translation

a) 开放式的公路收费是一种不设收费站的电子收费方式,其主要优点是用户可以驾车高速经过收费站而不需要减速来完成通行费支付。

b) 验证和收费是通过结合相机拍摄汽车和一个无线电频率键控计算机查找驾驶员窗口以及安装有感应器的保险杠来实施的。

c) 电子收费系统依赖于4个主要组件:自动车辆识别、自动车辆分类、交易事务处理、违章处理。

Chapter 3 Advanced Traveler Information Systems (ATIS)

3.1 Overview of ATIS

Ⅰ. True or false

a) F

b) F

c) T

d) T

e) F

Ⅱ. Filling blanks

a) traffic congestion

b) disseminated

c) traffic surveillance and control systems

d) origin-destination

e) innovative technologies

Ⅲ. Translation

a) 先进的出行者信息系统的主要功能是为不同种类的出行者,主要是为驾驶员和公共交通用户,在正确的时间和位置提供准确的交通信息。

b) GPS 数据首先通过源操作符接收,然后被转化为包括时间戳、GPS 设备标识、纬度、经度、航向(即方向)和瞬时速度等属性的多元组。

c) 大多数国家都有使用 IT 技术来解决不同交通问题的长期研究和开发经验。

3.2 Route Choice with Real-time Information

Ⅰ. True or false

a) F
b) T
c) T
d) F
e) T

Ⅱ. Filling blanks

a) productive
b) account for
c) stochastic
d) approximation
e) endeavor

Ⅲ. Translation

a) 从长期来看,这些系统可以减少建设额外的公路基础设施的需求,或者它们也可能引发新的额外需求。

b) 同时,随着传感器和通信技术的迅速发展,在这样一个非确定的系统中帮助出行者做出潜在更好的决策时,实时信息也变得更加可用。

c) 路由策略的定义是在当前时间和实时信息前提下,如何为当前结点提供下一步要到达的结点的规则,本质上是一个从网络状态到下一步结点决定的映射。

3.3 GIS and GPS in ITS

Ⅰ. True or false

a) F
b) T
c) F
d) T
e) T

Ⅱ. Filling blanks

a) combines with

b) dimension

c) veracity

d) ameliorate

e) facilities

Ⅲ. Translation

a) GPS 是一个基于卫星的导航、定位和授时系统。

b) 我们使用综合了 GPS 信号、车辆速度传感器、陀螺仪的应用来生成车辆的实时位置信息,并根据 GIS 电子地图把这些位置显示在屏幕上。

c) 公路状况、车道数目、速度限制和其他交通相关的信息在现实世界中经常改变。

Chapter 4　Advanced Vehicle Control Systems（AVCS）

4.1　Intelligent Vehicle Technology

Ⅰ. True or false

a) T

b) F

c) T

d) F

e) T

Ⅱ. Filling blanks

a) convenience

b) radar

c) Headway Advisory

d) degraded

e) intelligent speed adaptation

Ⅲ. Translation

a) 智能车辆系统被看作是超越现有的主动安全系统的下一代系统。现有系统提供了比较基础的控制辅助,但无法进行环境感知或风险评估。比如防抱死制动系统,牵引力控制系统,电子稳定控制系统都属于现有的主动安全系统。

b) 从根本上讲,便利系统是能帮助驾驶人控制车辆降低驾驶压力的驾驶支持产品。有时这些产品和安全性有关,因为驾驶人通常认为他们是安全系统,但在市场定位上它们却并不是安全系统。

c) 发生在发达国家的交通致命事故成千上万,碰撞事故更以数百万计。由于其巨大的社会成本,政府积极推进主动安全系统用于避免碰撞。

4.2　The Self-Driving Car

Ⅰ. True or false

a) F

b) T

c) F

d) F

e) T

Ⅱ. Filling blanks

a) Google Chauffeur

b) California

c) Toyota Prius

d) Stanford

e) reliability

Ⅲ. Translation

a) 当前,21世纪的前几十年,工业处于革命性变革的风口浪尖上——不仅在竞争格局上而且在与车辆交互的方式上将有潜力进行大的重塑,事实上还包括我们的道路和城市的未来设计。这次革命将随着自主或"自动驾驶"车辆的出现而发生,而且时间比你想象中更快。

b) 2011年6月内华达州通过了一项关于自动汽车运行的法律,将于2012年3月1日生效。采用谷歌的实验无人驾驶技术改动的丰田普锐斯在2012年5月通过了内华达州机动车管理部门的许可,这是美国颁发的第一个无人驾驶汽车许可证。

c) 该车还携带了其他的传感器,包括:安装在前后保险杠上的4个雷达,让车可以"看"到足够远以确保能处理高速路上的快速交通;一个安装在后视镜附近的摄像头,用于检测交通灯;还有GPS、惯性测量元件以及车轮编码器来确定车辆的位置及位置跟踪。

4.3 Automatic Parking System

Ⅰ. True or false

a) T

b) F

c) F

d) F

e) T

Ⅱ. Filling blanks

a) ultrasonic

b) Intelligent Parking Assist

c) Park Mate

d) Sweden

e) wireless

Ⅲ. Translation

a) 停车辅助系统的最简单形式是基于后置摄像头,可以提供汽车后方的视频图像,但没有感知和驾驶警告。视频图像显示在仪表控制台的屏幕上,该屏幕在车辆前行时作为导航显示屏。通常,当挂倒挡时车辆后方的图像会自动显示在屏幕上。通过这种方式,驾驶人可以看见后面的小物体并估算和墙、障碍物之间的距离。

b)对许多驾驶人来说,平行停车是个严峻的考验,由于大城市停车空间有限,因此如何将车停进狭小的空间是个重要的技能。这并不是件容易的事情,它可能导致车辆排队、神经紧张疲惫和挡泥板弯曲。幸运的是,技术给出了答案——汽车可以自动停车。想象一下,寻找完美的停车位,控制你的车来回移动,你只要按下按钮、坐下来、放松。同样的技术还可以用于防碰撞系统,最终可用于自主驾驶汽车上。

c)另一个即将到来的发展方向是采用无线技术将汽车之间连接起来。如果一辆车在弯道上检测到打滑的情况,它后面的车都将受到信息并减速。牵引力控制系统也将干涉车辆的运动。此外,系统将通过其他车的速度来检测交通路况并给出建议的替代路线。

Chapter 5　Advanced Public Transportation Systems（APTS）

5.1　Urban Transit Definitions

Ⅰ. True or false

a）T

b）F

c）T

d）F

e）T

Ⅱ. Filling blanks

a）culture and education

b）railway suburban passenger transport

c）driverless taxi system

d）large capacity／low energy consumption

e）shuttle buses

Ⅲ. Translation

a）城市运输系统是城市中乘客的公共承运商。

b）世界各国城市公共交通事业的发展进程,受本国经济和科学技术水平的影响,差异很大。

c）中小城市中一般以公共汽车、有轨电车、无轨电车等为主要客运工具,其特点是灵活机动,成本相对较低。

5.2　Public Transportation Priority

Ⅰ. True or false

a）F

b）F

c）T

d）T

e）T

Ⅱ. Filling blanks

a）capacity／speed

b) Separate rights of way

c) on board the bus

d) specialized design

e) traffic congestion

Ⅲ. Translation

a) 快速公交(BRT 或 BRTs)是一种基于公共交通的大众运输系统。

b) 禁止转弯是移动的公共汽车通过路口的最重要措施——比信号优先都更为重要。

c) 站台地面与公交车齐平可方便轮椅、残疾人乘客和婴儿车上下车,使延误降到最低。

5.3 Automatic Vehicle Location

Ⅰ. True or false

a) T

b) T

c) T

d) T

e) T

Ⅱ. Filling blanks

a) vehicle tracking system

b) SMS / GPRS

c) bandwidth

d) graded service

e) passenger information system

Ⅲ. Translation

a) 自动车辆定位(AVL)是一种自动确定和传输车辆的地理位置的方法。

b) 自动车辆定位是对服务车辆、急救车辆,特别是珍贵的建筑设备以及公共交通工具(公共汽车和火车)进行车队管理的一个强大理念。

c) 当管理车队时,了解所有驾驶人的实时位置可以更加有效地满足客户需求。

Chapter 6　Commercial Vehicle Operation Systems(CVOS)

6.1　Intelligence in Transport Logistics

Ⅰ. True or false

a) T

b) F

c) F

d) T

e) F

Ⅱ. Filling blanks

a) refers to

b) prompted

c) adoption

d) leading to

e) transmitting

Ⅲ. Translation

a) 运输涵盖整个生产过程,包括从生产到交付至最终消费者以及再从其返回的各个阶段。

b) 信息和通信技术在交通领域的应用促进了智能交通系统的产生。

c) 不同的技术,如智能交通信号灯,车牌识别摄像机,配备传感器的测速相机,以及可变交通信号标志等,被使用在交通信息系统中。

6.2　Challenges of CVOS

Ⅰ. True or false

a) F

b) T

c) T

d) F

e) T

Ⅱ. Filling blanks

a) organized

b) enrolled

c) significantly

d) includes

e) certified

Ⅲ. Translation

a) 通道通常是围绕一个主要公路,或公路系统,横跨几个区域或国家的司法管辖区。

b) 联邦汽车运输安全管理局(FMCSA)是按照1999年的汽车运输安全改进法案在美国运输部(USDOT)内部建立的一个执行管理部门。

c) 它是ITS大体系结构结构中的一部分,包括由政府、运营商和其他利益相关者拥有和操作的相关信息系统。

6.3　Electronic Screening System for the State of Missouri

Ⅰ. True or false

a) T

b) T

c) F

d) T

e) F

Ⅱ. Filling blanks

a) without

b) with

c) responsible
d) either
e) with

Ⅲ. Translation

a) 本文讲述下述内容：商用车辆营运的当前条件和密苏里州的通信基础设施；电子标签技术的讨论；提议中的密苏里州电子筛查系统的架构以及实施计划的当前状态。

b) 密苏里州建立了州一级的ITS/CVO常务委员会，它包含所有与商用车辆营运相关的机构。该委员会负责完成一份针对ITS/CVO的协议备忘录，该备忘录由以下机构的负责人签署：

（1）密苏里州交通局；
（2）密苏里州公路巡逻队；
（3）密苏里州税务局；
（4）密苏里州经济发展局；
（5）联邦公路管理局密苏里分局办公室；
（6）联邦公路管理局下属的公路运输办公室；
（7）密苏里州公路运输协会。

这份协议备忘录也由密苏里州长签署。

c) 当前的称重执法策略是在磅秤开放时所有的货车都被要求在称重站停车受检。这就导致了合法车辆不必要的延迟，同时所有货车的进出也可能导致安全隐患。目前，在不停车的状况下，不论在称重检测站还是路边的监测点都不能检查驾驶人和车辆的身份。不论运输过程是否合法都要停车受检，降低了执法的工作效率和运输的生产率。

Appendix

1 Acronym

A2A   Application to Application
ABS   Anti-lock Braking System
ADUS   Archived Data User Service
ADVANCE   Advanced Driver and Vehicle Advisory Navigation Concept
AFF   Application File Format
AHS   Automated Highway System
aka/AKA   also known as
AMASCOT   Automated Mileage and Stateline Crossing Operational Test
ANSI   American National Standards Institute
API   Application Processing Interface
APPN   Advanced Peer-to-Peer Networking
APTS   Advanced Public Transportation Systems
A&S   Architecture & Standards
ASN   Abstract Syntax Notation
ASP   Active Server Pages
ATIPE   Advanced Technologies for International and Intermodal Ports of Entry
ATIS   Advanced Traveler Information Systems
ATM   Asynchronous Transfer Mode
ATMS   Advanced Traffic/Management Systems
AVC   Automatic Vehicle Classification
AVCS   Advanced Vehicle Control Systems
AVCSS   Advanced Vehicle Control and Safety Systems
AVI   Automatic Vehicle Identification
AVL   Automatic Vehicle Location
BBS   Bulletin Board System
BIOS   Basic Input/Output System
BPR   Business Process Re-engineering
CA   Credentials Administration

CAD   Computer-Aided Dispatch
       Computer-Aided Design
CARS   Credentials Administration Requirements Specifications
CASE   Computer Aided Software Engineering
CAT   Carrier Automated Transaction
CCTV   Closed Circuit Television
CD   Compact Disk
CDL   Commercial Driver's License
CDLIS Commercial Driver's License Information System
CDPD   Cellular Digital Packet Data
CD-ROM   Compact Disk-Read Only Memory
CFR   Code of Federal Regulations
CH   Clearinghouse
CI   Credentialing Interface
CIO   Chief Information Officer
CIS   Credential Input System; Central Information Site
CM   Configuration Management
CMM   Capability Maturity Model
CMV   Commercial Motor Vehicle
COVE   Commercial Vehicle
CPM   Critical Path Method
CR   Compliance Review
       Change Request
CRF   Change Request Form
CUSDEC   Customs Declaration
CUSRES   Customs Response Message
CV   Commercial Vehicle
CVIEW Commercial Vehicle Information Exchange Window
CVIS   Commercial Vehicle Information System
CVISN Commercial Vehicle Information Systems and Networks
CVL   Commercial Vehicle Licensing
CVO   Commercial Vehicle Operations
CY   Calendar Year
DARPA Defense Advanced Research Projects Agency
DB   Database
DBA   Doing Business As
DHCP   Dynamic Host Configuration Protocol
DL   Drivers License
DMV   Department of Motor Vehicles
DNA   Digital Network Architecture

DOB   Date of Birth
DOL   Department of Licensing
DOS   Disk Operating System
DOT   Department of Transportation
DSRC   Dedicated Short Range Communication
DSSSL   Document Style Semantics and Specification Language
e-   electronic (e.g., e-mail, e-screening)
EDI   Electronic Data Interchange
EDIFACT   EDI For Administration, Commerce, and Transport
EDL   Electronic Data Library
EEOS   Electronic One-Stop Shopping
EFT   Electronic Funds Transfer
ePC   Electronic Product Code
ES   Electronic Screening (e-screening)
ESD   Electronic Security Device
ESE   Electronic Screening (E-Screening) Enrollment
ETC   Electronic Toll Collection
ETTM   Electronic Toll and Traffic Management
FAA   Federal Aviation Administration
FAQ   Frequently Asked Questions
FCC   Federal Communications Commission
FDDI   Fiber Distributed Data Interface
FEIN   Federal Employer Identification Number
FMS   Fleet Management System
FOC   Final Operating Capability
FP2FP   Fixed Point to Fixed Point
FSR   Feasibility Study Report
FTP   File Transfer Protocol
FY   Fiscal Year
GCWR   Gross Combination Weight Rating
GIF   Graphics Interchange Format
GIS   Geographical Information System
GMT   Greenwich Meridian/Mean Time
GPS   Global Positioning System
GSM   Global Systems for Mobile Communications
GUI   Graphical User Interface
GVW   Gross Vehicle Weight
GVWR   Gross Vehicle Weight Rating
HAZMAT   Hazardous Material
HDDV   Heavy Duty Diesel Vehicle

HM   Hazardous Material
HOS   Hours of service
HOV   High Occupancy Vehicle
HQ   Headquarters
HSWIM   High Speed Weigh-In-Motion
HTML   HyperText Markup Language
HTTP   Hypertext Transfer Protocol
HTTPS   Hypertext Transfer Protocol-Secure
IACP   International Association of Chiefs of Police
IBC   International Border Clearance
IBEX   International Border Electronic Crossing
IBM   International Business Machine
ICD   Interface Control Document
ID/IQ   Indefinite Delivery / Indefinite Quantity
IEEE   Institute of Electrical and Electronics Engineers
IEN   Information Exchange Network
IES   Information Exchange System
I/F   Interface
IFTA   International Fuel Tax Agreement
IG   Implementation Guide
IMS   Information Management Systems
I/O   Input/Output
IP   Internet Protocol
IPSec   Internet Protocol Security
IR   Inter-regional; Infrared
IRP   International Registration Plan
IS   Information System(s)
ISDN   Integrated Services Digital Network
ISO   International Standards Organization
ISP   Internet Service Provider
IT   Information Technology
ITS   Intelligent Transportation Systems (formerly IVHS)
ITS-A   Intelligent Transportation Systems - America
IVHS   Intelligent Vehicle-Highway System
IVI   Intelligent Vehicle Initiative
JPEG   Joint Photographics Expert Group
KB   Kilobyte
LAN   Local Area Network
LPR   License Plate Reader
MAN   Metropolitan Area Network

MDT	Mobile Data Terminal
MHz	Megahertz
MOA	Memorandum of Agreement
MOE	Measure Of Effectiveness
MPEG	Moving Picture Experts Group
NA	Not Applicable (also N/A)
NOI	Notice Of Investigation
NSF	National Science Foundation
NT	New Technology (Microsoft Operating System)
OBC	On-Board Computer
OCD	Operational Concept Document
OIC	Office in Charge
O&M	Operations & Maintenance
OMC	Office of Motor Carriers
OOS	Out of Service
OOSD	Out of Service Driver
OOSV	Out of Service Vehicle
Op-Model	Operational Model
OS/OW	Oversize/Overweight
PC	Personal Computer
PDA	Personal Data Assistant
PIN	Personal Identification Number
POE	Port of Entry
POP	Post Office Protocol
PPTP	Point-to-Point Tunneling Protocol
PR	Proposed Recommendation
QA	Quality Assurance
RAID	Redundant Array of Independent Disks
RDF	Resource Description Format
REC	W3C Recommendation
RES	Roadside Electronic Screening
RF	Radio Frequency
RFID	Radio Frequency Identification
RFP	Request for Proposal
RFQ	Request for Quote
ROC	Roadside Operations Computer
RWIS	Road Weather Information System
RYG	Red, Yellow, Green
SAE	Society of Automotive Engineers
SAFER	Safety and Fitness Electronic Records

SafeStat Safety Status
SDS Safety Data Systems
SE Southeastern States
SGML Standard Generalized Markup Language
SHRP
SMTP Simple Mail Transfer Protocol
SNA Systems Network Architecture
SNET SAFETYNET
SOAP Simple Object Access Protocol
SQL Structured Query Language
SSN Social Security Number
SVC Service
TBD To Be Determined
TCAM Telecommunications Access Method
TCP/IP Transmission Control Protocol/Internet Protocol
TIN Tax Identification Number
TPM Technical Performance Measure
TZ Time Zone
UML Unified Modeling Language
UDP User Datagram Protocol
URI Uniform Resource Identifier
URL Universal Resource Locator
USDOT United States Department of Transportation
V&V Verification and Validation
V2R Vehicle-to-Roadside
V2V Vehicle-to-Vehicle
VAN Value-Added Network
VIN Vehicle Identification Number
VPN Virtual Private Network
W3C World Wide Web Consortium
WAN Wide Area Network
WBS Work Breakdown Structure
WD Working Draft
WECI Web-Enabled Credentialing Interface
WG Working Group
WiFi Wireless Fidelity
WIM Weigh-In-Motion
WMI World Manufacturer Identifier
WWW World Wide Web
XHTML eXtensible Hypertext Markup Language

XML eXtensible Markup Language
XQL XML Query Language
XSL eXtensible Stylesheet Language
XSLT eXtensible Stylesheet Language Transformations
Y2K Year 2000

2 Glossary

ACC (Adaptive Cruise Control):
Cruise control system that uses sensors to automatically maintain a safe distance from the vehicle ahead, adapting to speed changes, etc.

ADAS (Advanced Driver Assistance Systems):
In-vehicle technologies designed to improve vehicle safety by aiding the driver, such as collision avoidance, curve warning, distance control, etc.

AFS (Advanced Frontline System):
concept of intelligent lighting, according to curves, weather and speed

AHS (Automated Highway System):
research initiative aimed at developing automatic guidance on motorways for vehicles using cruise control

AID (Automatic Incident Detection):
radar- or video-controlled system enabling rapid location of an incident or accident on tunnels and motorways

ALERT (Advice and problem Location for European Road Traffic):
protocol used for traffic messages by RDS-TMC

Alpha Version:
an early testing, pre-release version of a program, which may still have bugs, or features that do not work.

AMI-C (Automotive Multimedia Interface Consortium):
Non-profit corporation of worldwide vehicle manufacturers which aims to develop a set of common specifications for a multimedia interface to motor vehicle electronic systems to accommodate a variety of computer-based electronic devices in the vehicle.

ANSI (American National Standards Institute):
The primary organization for fostering the development of technology standards in the United States. ANSI works with industry groups and is the U. S. member of the International Organization for Standardization (ISO) and the International Electrotechnical Commission (IEC).

API (Application Programming Interfaces):
The specific method prescribed by a computer operating system or by an application program by which a programmer writing an application program can make requests of the operating system or another application. (sometimes called application*programming* interface).

ASIC:
Application Specific Integrated Circuit

AVC (Automatic Vehicle Classification):
a method for classifying trucks by vehicle length, number of axles, and axle spacing

AVI (Automated Vehicle Identification):
a system which transmits signals from an on-board tag or transponder to roadside receivers for uses such as electronic toll collection (ETC) and stolen vehicle recovery

AVL (Automated Vehicle Location):
location system, in particular for buses and heavy-goods vehicles, used widely in fleet management utilizing technologies such as GSM, GPS and Internet

BAS (Brake Assist System):
safety system amplifying the brake force in case of emergency

Beta Version:
A test-release version of a program which has been fairly well debugged and tested (compared to the alpha version), but is not yet considered complete because of missing features.

CAN (Controlled Area Network):
data bus which enables computerised exchanges in a high bandwidth

CEN (Comité Européen de Normalisation):
European Standardisation Committee

DAB (Digital Audio Broadcasting):
standard which enables the high-quality transmission of text, data and sound at a higher data rate

DARC (Data Radio Channel):
adigital data transmission method using FM radio that is compatible with RDS and offers a higher bit rate (10 kbits/s)

DATEX (Data Exchange Network):
agreement between European traffic centres to exchange traffic and travel information

Digital Tachograph:
an electronic system fitted to commercial vehicles to record driver information and details about driving time and distance

DSRC (Dedicated Short Range Communication):
Standard enabling data transmission at a frequency of 5.8 GHz, which is used to identify a vehicle, store and transfer screening data, and signal the driver of the pull-in decision. DSRC is used to provide data communications between a moving vehicle and the roadside equipment by means of a transponder ("tag") mounted in the cab of the vehicle, and a reader and antenna at the roadside.

EC:
European Commission

EDI (Electronic Data Interchange):
a standard form of electronic communication used mainly for electronic commerce and document interchange

EFC (Electronic Fee Collection):

a system that enables automatic debiting/payment for a transport service without any action from the user at the moment of use - example: automatic toll collection

ESP (Electronic Stability Program):

safety function linked to brake sensors and traction control which enables cars to correct their trajectory on slippery roads and curves

FCD (Floating Car Data):

Floating car data are gathered from vehicles equipped with appropriate sensors (such as whether windscreen wipers are activated or the vehicle's location and speed) and then passed to traffic management centres that can evaluate this information for general traffic trends.

Galileo:

the European contribution to the Global Navigation Satellite System; full operational capability planned for 2008

GATS (Global Automotive Telematics Standard):

open standard to enable a full range of traffic information and other telematics services

GIS (Geographic Information Systems):

a computerized data management system designed to capture, store, retrieve, analyze, and report geographic and demographic information

GNSS (Global Navigation Satellite System):

the combined total of all satellite navigation and positioning systems operating around the world and offering signal reception worldwide

GPRS (General Packet Radio Service):

standard for data transmission by packet, with a speed of 64 Kbits/s

GPS (Global Positioning System):

a U.S. space-based radio-navigation system that provides reliable positioning, navigation, and timing services to civilian users on a continuous worldwide basis—freely available to all

GSM (Global System for Mobile Communications):

digital cellular telephony system used in ITS services such as traffic information, emergency call and fleet management

HMI (Human Machine Interface):

previously know as man-machine interface (MMI); means by which a user interacts with a machine and includes simple and advanced functions such as voice recognition, speech synthesis and touch screens

Intermodality:

The ability to move between two or more modes of transport

IR:

Infrared

ISA (Intelligent Speed Adaptation):

systems designed to alert drivers when they exceed the speed limit or are travelling dangerously slow, with some systems also offering dynamic correction capabilities

ISO (International Standards Organization):

An international organization composed of national standards bodies from over 75 countries. ⋯ ISO has defined a number of important computer standards, the most significant of which is perhaps OSI (Open Systems Interconnection), a standardized architecture for designing networks.

ITS (Intelligent Transport Systems and Services):

any system or service that makes the movement of people or goods more efficient and economical, thus more "intelligent"

LBS (Location-Based Services):

services that depend on knowing the user's location to deliver user-specific information, such as real-time traffic updates or point-of-interest data

MAGIC (Mobile Automotive Geographic Information Core):

an industry consortium established to develop and promote an open industry specification for delivering navigation, telematics and related geographic information services across multiple networks, platforms, and devices

MOST Cooperation:

cooperation between car manufacturers and OEM suppliers to develop a low cost, high bandwidth solution for data and multimedia in-vehicle applications

OBU:

On-Board Unit

PC:

Personal Computer

PDA (Personal Digital Assistant):

small, hand-held devices offering functions similar to a personal computer (though limited); also now offering access to some ITS services

RDS (Radio Data System):

digital channel transmitted within the FM radio wavelength used to relay traffic messages

RDS-TMC:

Radio Data Systems incorporating a Traffic Message Channel

Road pricing:

use of smart card technology or simple tags to charge road users based on criteria such as demand, congestion, time, or distance

SMS:

Short Messsage Service

Telematics:

combination of telecommunications and informatics

TMC (Traffic Message Channel):

digital channel used to provide silent, coded messages to in-vehicle applications in order to display route and traffic information in a user's native language

UMTS (Universal Mobile Telecommunication System):

standard for third-generation digital cellular telephony which enables users to receive video and audio on mobile phones

VMS(Variable Message Signs):

roadside message displays used for traffic control and information

WAP(Wireless Application Protocol):

standard which brings Internet content to mobile phones

WIM(Weigh In Motion):

a technology for determining the weight of a commercial vehicle without requiring it to stop on a scale, using AVI to identify the vehicles and other technologies to measure the dynamic tire forces of a moving vehicle and then estimate the corresponding static weight

XFCD:

Extended Floating Car Data

3　Grammar

一、动词的时态

时态是一种动词形式,不同的时态用以表示不同的时间与方式,是表示行为、动作和状态在各种时间条件下的动词形式。

时态不同,变化形式也不同。以 do 为例,列表如下:

	一般	进行	完成	完成进行
现在时	does, do	am/is/are + doing	has/have + done	has/have + been doing
过去时	did	was/were + doing	had + done	had been + doing
将来时	shall/will + do	shall/will be + doing	shall/will have + done	shall/will have been doing
过去将来时	should/would + do	would/should + be doing	should/would + have done	would/should + have been doing

下面主要介绍其中五种时态的构成及用法。

1. 一般现在时

(1)构成:通常以动词原形表示。如主语为第三人称单数,动词要改为第三人称单数形式。否定句或疑问句要借助于助动词 does。

	be	行为动词
肯定句	主语 + be + 表语	主语 + do/does
否定句	主语 + be + not + 表语	主语 + don't/doesn't + do sth.
一般疑问句	Be + 主语 + 表语	Do/Does + 主语 + do sth.?
特殊疑问句	What + be + 主语 + 表语	What + do/does + 主语 + do + sth.?
时间状语	often, every day, usually	

(2)例句:

My father drives to his office. 我父亲开车去上班。

We usually go to work by bus, but today by subway. 我们通常坐公交车去上班,但是今天坐地铁去的。

2. 现在进行时

(1)构成:由助动词 be + 现在分词构成。其中 be 有人称和数的变化。

肯定句	主语 + am/is/are + 现在分词
否定句	主语 + am/is/are not + 现在分词
一般疑问句	Am/Is/Are + 主语 + 现在分词?
特殊疑问句	What + am/is/are + 主语 + 现在分词?
时间状语	Now, at 10 a.m., at the moment

(2)例句：

We are having English class right now. 我们现在正在上英语课。

He is doing his homework. 他正在做作业。

3. 现在完成时

(1)构成：由助动词 have + 过去分词构成，助动词 have 有人称和数的变化。第三人称单数用 has，其余用 have。

肯定句	主语 + have/has + 过去分词
否定句	主语 + have/has not + 过去分词
一般疑问句	Have/Has + 主语 + 过去分词?
特殊疑问句	What + have/has + 主语 + 过去分词?
时间状语	already, ever, yet, just

(2)例句：

I have already told you that. 我已经告诉过你了。

We haven't seen her recently. 最近我们没有见到她。

4. 一般过去时

(1)构成：一般过去时通常又动词过去式表示。一般过去式的否定式、疑问是和简单回答形式要用助动词 do 的过去式 did，同事注意实义动词要用原形。

	be	行为动词
肯定句	主语 + was/were + 表语	主语 + 过去式
否定句	主语 + was/were not + 表语	主语 + didn't + 动词原形
一般疑问句	Was/Were + 主语 + 表语	Did + 主语 + 动词原形?
特殊疑问句	特殊疑问词 + was/were + 主语 + 表语	特殊疑问词 + did + 主语 + 动词原形?
时间状语	yesterday, last month, in 1998	

(2)例句：

What time did you get up yesterday morning? 昨天早上你什么时候起床的?

They were very happy at the party last week. 上周的聚会上他们很开心。

5. 一般将来时

(1)构成：shall/will + 动词原形，第一人称 I、we 用 shall 或 will，其余用 will。

肯定句	主语 + will/shall + 动词原形
否定句	主语 + will/shall not + 动词原形
一般疑问句	Will/Shall + 主语 + 动词原形?
特殊疑问句	What + will/shall + 主语 + 动词原形?
时间状语	next year, tomorrow, in the future

(2)例句:

He will pick you up at the station tomorrow morning. 明天早上他在车站接你。

I won't tell you my secret. 我不会告诉你我的秘密。

二、被动语态

被动语态的基本形式是:(助动词适当形式)be + done(动词的过去分词)用于被动语态的动词主要是及物动词。被动语态的句子就是把主动语态句子中的宾语变成了主语,谓语采用被动语态结构,将主动语态中的主语放到了句末,前面加介词 by。

例:This picture *was taken* by a young reporter in Beijing last month. 这幅照片由一名年轻记者上个月在北京拍摄。

主动语态与被动语态的句子比较:

主动语态(Active)	被动语态(Passive)
They *broke* the rules.	The rules *were broken*.
We *are repairing* the road.	The road *is being repaired*.
The machine *can do* this.	This *can be done* by the machine.
You *must shut* these windows.	These windows *must be shut*.
They *should have told* her.	She *should have been told*.

三、形容词和副词的比较级和最高级

多数形容词和副词有比较级和最高级的变化,即原级、比较级和最高级,用来表示事物的等级差别。原级即形容词的原形,比较级和最高级由规则变化和不规则变化两种。

1. 规则变化

(1)单音节词和少数双音节词,加词尾-er, -est 来构成比较级和最高级。如:high- higher-highest。

(2)以不发音 e 结尾的词,直接加-r, -st。如:late-later-latest。

(3)词尾是"短元音 + 辅音"时,应双写结尾的辅音字母,再加-er, -est。如:thin-thinner-thinnest。

(4)词尾是"辅音字母 + y"时,讲 y 变为 i 再加-er, -est。如:heavy-heavier-heaviest。

(5)通常以-ful, -less, -ish 等结尾的双音节词和多音节词,在词前加 more, most。如:different-more different-the most different。

例:Breaks should not be longer than the time allowed. 休息时间不得超过规定时间。

2. 常见不规则变化

good/well-better-best

bad/ill-worse-worst

many/much-more-most

little-less-least

far(表示距离)-farther-farthest

far(表示程度)-further-furthest

3. 形容词、副词比较级和最高级的句型

(1)A 近似或相当于 B。A + 谓语 + as + 形容词或副词原级 + as + B(在否定句或疑问句中可用 so...as)。

例：Skiing is as interesting as skateboarding. 滑雪和滑板运动一样有趣。

(2)A 剩余 B(A 不等于 B)；A + 谓语 + 比较级 + than B。

例：Facts speak louder than eloquence. 事实胜于雄辩。

(3)The...the...结构(表示"越……就越……")；The + 形容词或副词比较级(+ 主语 + 谓语),the + 形容词或副词比较级(+ 主语 + 谓语)。

例：The more she knows, the smarter she is. 她知道得越多越聪明。

(4)形容词比较级 + 形容词比较级(表示"越来越……")；主语 + 谓语 + 比较级 + 比较级。

例：The boy is getting taller and taller. 男孩越长越高。

(5)形容词或副词表示倍数的常见句型(表示 A 是 B 的 N 倍)。

A is N times as great (long, much,...) as B.

A is N times greater (longer, more,...) than B.

A is N times the size (length, amount,...) of B.

例：The room is twice as big as my office.

The room is twice bigger than my office.

The room is twice the size of my office.

这房间比我的办公室大两倍。

四、定语从句

定语从句在复合句中充当定语,作用相当于形容词,用来修饰主句中的某一名词或代词或整个主句,所以也称作形容词性从句。定语从句由关联词引出,而且一般紧跟在它所修饰的先行词之后。关系代词有 that、which、who、whom、whose、as 关系副词有 when、where、why。

1. 限制性定语从句

限制性定语从句是先行词在意义上不可缺少的定语,是不能去掉的。如果将限制性定语从句去掉,剩下部分的意思就不清楚或失去意义。

例：This is the girl *whom they interviewed this morning*. 这就是今天早上他们采访的那个女孩。

2. 非限制性定语从句

非限制性定语从句在意义上只是起到附加说明的作用,因此当把非限制性定语从句删掉时,其余部分的意思仍然清楚完整。

例：New Concept English is intended for foreign students, *which is known to us all*. 新概念英语是专为外国学生编写的,这是我们大家都知道的。

五、状语从句

状语从句是指句子用作状语时起副词作用的句子。状语从句由从属连词引导,可以表示时间、地点、原因、条件、让步、方式、目的、结果、比较等含义。不同的状语从句由不同的连接词,而且都有其特定的意义。

下面列举一些常见的状语从句。

1. 时间状语从句

常用的连词有 when、whenever、as、since、till/until、before、after、as soon as、the moment、no sooner...than(一……就……)、hardly...when...、the instant、the minute、every time、the second。

例：Tell me *whenever* you need me. 无论什么时候需要我,请告诉我。

No sooner had she got off the train *than* her husband ran towards her. 她刚一下车,她丈夫就向她跑过来。

2. 地点状语从句

地点状语从句由 where、wherever、everywhere 引导,可以放在主句前,也可以放在主句后。Where 指"某个地方",wherever 指"在任何一个地方",everywhere 指"到处"。

例:*Wherever* you go, you should do your work well. 无论你到什么地方都要把工作做好。

3. 原因状语从句

because 表示原因语气最强,常用于回答以疑问词 why 引导的疑问句。for 引导的从句并不说明主句行为发生的直接原因,只是提供一些有助于说明情况的补充说明,且不能位于主句前。since 表示一种附带的原因,或者表示已知的、显然的理由,意为"既然",引导从句通常放在句首。as 所表示的理由最弱,只是对主句的附带说明,重点在主句。as 从句通常放在主句前。

例:He was punished *because* he did not obey the regulations. 他受了处分,因为他没有遵守规定。

There must be no one in the house *for* the door is closed. 门关着,屋子里准是没人。(表示推断,不能用 because)

Since they say so, I suppose it is true. 既然他们这么说,我想这是真的。

As I am about to start a journey, I shall not be able to begin the project before I return. 因为我即将出去旅行,回来之前我不能开始那个项目。

4. 让步状语从句

常用连词:though、although(虽然)、even if(即使)、even though、while(尽管)、no matter what/how/which/who(不管什么/怎样/哪个/谁)、whatever(无论什么)、however(无论多么)、whichever(无论哪个)、whether...or not(无论…与否)、as(虽然)。

例:She had a very good time *although* she didn't know anybody at the party. 尽管在这次聚会上她谁都不认识,但她还是玩得很愉快。

No matter what happens, they shall never lose hope. 无论发生什么,他们都不会失去信心。

5. 条件状语从句

If 表示正面的条件"如果";unless 表示反面的条件,意为"除非,如果不"(=if...not)。

例:*If* she doesn't come before 10 o'clock, we won't wait for her. 如果她十点前不来,我们就不等她了。

I shall go tomorrow unless it rains. 除非明天下雨,否则我就要走了。

六、名词性从句

1. 宾语从句

宾语从句是在复合句中充当动词或介词宾语的从句。

(1)作动词宾语:从句跟在及物动词之后,表示动作的内容。

例:The tour guide <u>told</u> us when the bridge had been destroyed by earthquake. 导游给我们讲述了这座桥是何时被大火烧毁的。

(2)作介词的宾语。

例:They are talking <u>about</u> what the boy said just now. 他们正在谈论那个男孩刚才所讲的事情。

(3)某些形容词后的宾语从句。

例:We are sure that we shall succeed.我们确信我们会成功。

2.同位语从句

同位语从句是在复合句中充当同位语的名词性从句,它是用来补充说明或解释它前面名词的内容。

同位语从句一般跟在某些名词后面,用以说明该名词表示的具体内容,同位语从句前的名词通常用单数形式,并且往往带有限定词(word 除外)加以修饰,可以跟同位语从句的名词通常有 news、idea、fact、promise、question、doubt、though、hope、message、suggestion、word(消息)、possibility 等。

例:I've come from Mr. Wang with the message that he won't be able to see you this morning.我从王先生那里来,他让我告诉你他今天上午不能来看你了。

I had no idea what has happened to her.我们不知道她出了什么事。

3.表语从句

表语从句时在复合句中作表语的名词性从句。可接表语从句的系动词有 be、look、seem、sound、appear、remain 等。引导表语从句的关联词由 that、what、who、when、where、which、why、whether、how、as、as if/though 等。表语从句一定要用陈述语序;不可以用 if,而用 whether 连接表语从句(as if 例外);不像宾语从句,在有表语从句的复合句中,主句时态和从句时态可以不一致;that 在表语从句中不可以省略掉。

例:It looked as if she had understood this question.看起来她好像已经明白了这个问题。

The question is whether the enemy is marching towards us.问题是敌人是否正朝着我方行进。

The question is who will travel with me to New York tomorrow.问题是明天谁会和我一起去纽约旅行。

What I told her was that I would help her with the housework.我告诉她的是我会帮她做家务。

七、虚拟语气

虚拟语气是通过特殊的谓语动词形式来表达的愿望、假设、怀疑、猜测或建议等语气,它不表示客观存在。

1.虚拟语气用于条件状语从句。

以下表格是虚拟语气用于条件状语从句中时,主句和从句谓语动词的形式:

	条件状语从句	主句
与过去事实相反	had + 过去分词	should/would/could/might + have + 过去分词
与现在事实相反	一般过去时(be 用 were)	should/would/could/might + 动词原形
与将来事实相反	一般过去时或 should(were to) + 动词原形	should/would/could/might + 动词原形

例:If you had taken my advice, you would have succeeded in the competition.如果你采纳了我的建议,你就赢得比赛了。

If I were a boy, I would join the army.如果我是个男孩,我就去参军。

If it were to rain tomorrow, the sports meeting would be put off.如果明天下雨的话,运动会就会推迟。

2.虚拟语气用于宾语从句

(1)"wish+宾语从句"表示不能实现的愿望,译为"要是……就好了"等。

例:I wish I could fly like a bird. 要是我能像小鸟一样飞就好了。

(2)在表示建议、要求、命令等动词后的宾语从句中,如 suggest、advise、propose、demand、require、insist、request、command、order 等,谓语动词用 should + 动词原形或是动词原形。

例:He suggest we(should)leave here at once. 他提议我们应马上离开这儿。

3.虚拟语气用于同位语从句和表语从句

作表示建议、要求、命令等的名词,如 advise、idea、order、demand、plan、proposal、suggestion、request 等的表语从句和同位语从句,从句中的谓语动词用"(should)+动词原形"。

例:My idea is that they(should)pay 100 dollars.

4.虚拟语气用于主语从句。

在主语从句中,谓语动词的虚拟语气用"should+动词原形"的结构,表示惊奇、不相信、理应如此等。

例:It is necessary(important,natural,strange,etc.)that we should clean the office every day. 我们每天打扫办公室是很有必要的(很重要的、很自然的、很奇怪的,等等)。

References

[1] Jesse H. Ausubel, Cesare Marchetti. The Evolution of Transport[J]. The Industrial Physicist, 2001, 7(2):20-24.

[2] The Intelligent Transportation Society of America (ITS America). ITS America's Strategic Plan [EB/OL]. [2014-09-14]. http://www.itsa.org/images/ITS%20America%20Strategic%20Plan_Final.pdf.

[3] IEEE Intelligent Transportation Systems Society (ITSS). About[EB/OL]. [2014-09-14]. http://sites.ieee.org/itss/about/.

[4] European Union (EU). Directive 2010/40/EU of the European Parliament and of the Council of 7 July 2010 on the framework for the deployment of Intelligent Transport Systems in the field of road transport and for interfaces with other modes of transport[J/S/OL]. Official Journal of the European Union, L 207, 2010,53:1-13[2014-09-14]. http://eur-lex.europa.eu/legal-content/EN/TXT/? uri = CELEX:32010L0040.

[5] ERTICO (ITS Europe). ITS can help improve our daily lives[EB/OL]. [2014-03-31]. http://www.ertico.com/about-ertico-its/.

[6] ITS Japan. What is ITS? [EB/OL]. [2014-03-31]. http://www.its-jp.org/english/about_e/what/.

[7] 中国智能交通协会. Background[EB/OL]. [2014-03-31]. http://www.itschina.org/article.asp? articleid =499.

[8] Transport Department, the Government of the Hong Kong Special Administrative Region of PRC. Intelligent Transport Systems (ITS)[EB/OL]. [2014-03-31]. http://www.td.gov.hk/en/transport_in_hong_kong/its/.

[9] The Japan Organizing Committee of ITS WORLD CONGRESS TOKYO 2013. Final official statistics on ITS WORLD CONGRESS TOKYO 2013 are posted[EB/OL]. (2014-01-27) [2014-03-31]. http://www.itsworldcongress.jp/photo_gallery/index.html

[10] Marsh Products, INC. Vehicle Detection Products[EB/OL]. [2014-03-31]. http://www.marshproducts.com/vehicle.htm.

[11] Natasha Jones. Police question traffic control costs[N/OL]. Aldergrove Star (2011-02-17) [2014-03-31]. http://www.aldergrovestar.com/news/116429969.html.

[12] Zabi Kator. Why Use Traffic Control Security Guard Services? [R/OL]. (2013-01-18) [2014-03-31]. http://www.guardnow.com/blog/why-use-traffic-control-security-guard-

services/.

[13] Kapsch TrafficCom AB, Kapsch Telecom GmbH and Thales e-Transactions CGA SA. GSS, Global specification for short range communication: the platform for interoperable electronic toll collection and access control[S/OL]. Version 3.2, August 2003[2014-09-14]. http://profesores.elo.utfsm.cl/~agv/elo326/1s06/ETC/GSS_32.pdf.

[14] S C WONG. Development of GIS – based advanced traveler information system (ATIS) in Hong Kong[D]. Hong Kong University, Master Thesis, 2002.

[15] A Biem, E Bouillet, H H Feng, et al. IBM inforsphere streams for scalabel realtime intelligent transportation services[C]. In ACM SIGMOD/PODS Conference, 6th-11th, Indiana, 2010.

[16] B E Eran, R D Pace, G N Bifulco, et al. Modelling the impacts of ATIS accuracy on travellers' route – choice behavior and risk perception[C]. In European Transport Conference, Glasgow, UK, 11th-13th, October, 2010.

[17] Song Gao. Modeling Strategic Route Choice and Real-Time Information Impacts in Stochastic and Time-Dependent Networks[J]. IEEE Transactions on Intelligent Transportation Systems, 2012, 13(3):1298-1311.

[18] X K Zhou, M Chen, Y C Fu, et al. The application of GIS and GPS in ITS[C]. In International Conference on Convergence Information Technology, 21st-23rd, Nov, 2007.

[19] Richard Bishop. Intelligent vehicle technology and trends[M]. Artech House Publishers, 2005.

[20] Gary Silberg, Richard Wallace. Self – driving cars: The next revolution[R/OL]. August 2012[2014-09-14]. http://cargroup.org/?module=Publications&event=View&pubID=87.

[21] Wikipedia. Google driverless car[R/OL]. 2014-2-13[2014-2-15]. http://en.wikipedia.org/wiki/Google_driverless_car.

[22] Erico Guizzo. How Google's Self – Driving Car Works[R/OL]. 2011-10-18[2014-2-15]. http://spectrum.ieee.org/automaton/robotics/artificial–intelligence/how-google-self-driving-car-works.

[23] Self – Driving Cars. Technology Review[R/OL]. 2012-11[2014-2-15]. 115(6):41. Available from: Business Source Premier.

[24] Ed Grabianowski. How Self – parking Cars Work[R/OL]. [2014-02-15] http://auto.howstuffworks.com/car-driving-safety/safety-regulatory-devices/self-parking-car1.htm.

[25] Ho Gi Jung, Dong Suk Kim, Pal Joo Yoon, et al Parking Slot Markings Recognition for Automatic Parking Assist System[C]. Intelligent Vehicles Symposium 2006, 106-113, 13-15, Tokyo, Japan.

[26] Macro Corporation. The State of Arizona. Arizona Phase II Final Report: Statewide Radio Interoperability Needs Assessment[R], 2004. 165.

[27] Jeff Schaengold. Fuel theft in the USA reaches $8 Billion in 2008[R/OL]. [2014-09-14]. http://www.rfidsb.com/tm/2008/04/24/fuel-theft-in-the-usa-reaches-8-billion-in-2008/.

[28] Yung – yu Tseng, Wen Long Yue, Michael A P Taylor. The Role of Transportation in Logis-

tics Chain[C]. the Proceedings of the Eastern Asia Society for Transportation Studies, 2005, 5:1657-1672.

[29] Bernhard Tilanus. Information Systems in Logistics and Transportation[M]. Emerald Group Publishing Limited, UK, 1997.

[30] Organization for Economic Co-operation and Development (OECD). Transport Logistics: Shared Solutions to Common Challenges[M/OL], (2002-08-05)[2014-09-14]. http://www.dx.doi.org/10.1787/9789264171190-en.

[31] T G Crainic, M Gendreau, J Y Potvin. Intelligent freight-transportation systems: Assessment and the contribution of operations research[J]. Transportation Research Part C, 2009, 17: 541-557.

[32] V Mirzabeiki. An Overview of the Freight Intelligent Transportation Systems[C]. Proceedings of the 17th Intelligent Transportation Systems (ITS) World Congress, Busan, South Korea, 2010.

[33] Federal Motor Carrier Safety Administration, U.S. Department of Transportation. The Commercial Vehicle Information Systems and Networks Program CY 2011 Annual Report[R], January 2013.

[34] Federal Motor Carrier Safety Administration, U.S. Department of Transportation. Commercial Vehicle Information Systems and Networks (CVISN)[EB/OL]. [2014-09-14]. http://www.fmcsa.dot.gov/commercial-vehicle-information-systems-and-networks-cvisn.

[35] Federal Motor Carrier Safety Administration, U.S. Department of Transportation. CVISN Guides[EB/OL]. [2014-03-31]. http://cvisn.fmcsa.dot.gov/default.aspx?PageID=guides.

[36] K E Richeson. Introductory Guide to CVISN[R]. POR-99-7186, Preliminary Version P.2, The Johns Hopkins University Applied Physics Laboratory, February 2000.

[37] CVISN Guide to Safety Information Exchange[R]. POR-99-7191, Baseline Version V1.0, The Johns Hopkins University Applied Physics Laboratory, February 2002.

[38] CVISN Guide to Credentials Administration[R]. POR-99-7192, Preliminary Version P.2, The Johns Hopkins University Applied Physics Laboratory, August 2000.

[39] CVISN Guide to Electronic Screening[R]. POR-99-7193, Baseline Version 1.0, The Johns Hopkins University Applied Physics Laboratory, March 2002.

[40] Bill McCall, Marilyn Kuntemeyer. Commercial Vehicle Operations (CVO) Electronic Screening System for the State of Missouri-Implementation through Current ITS Technologies [C]. ITS America Seventh Annual Meeting, June 2-5, 1997, Washington, D.C. [2014-03-31]. http://www.ctre.iastate.edu/pubs/conferences/mccall/.

[41] CVISN Glossary[R]. POR-96-6997 V2.0, Baseline Version, The Johns Hopkins University Applied Physics Laboratory, December 2000[2014-03-31]. http://cvisn.fmcsa.dot.gov/downdocs/cvisndocs/1_general/glossv20.doc.

[42] CVISN Glossary[R]. NSTD-08-0717 V3.0. The Johns Hopkins University Applied Physics Laboratory, November 2008[2014-03-31]. http://www.fmcsa.dot.gov/documents/cvisn/deployment/CVISN-Glossary-V3.pdf.

[43] ERTICO (ITS Europe). Glossary[EB/OL].[2014-03-31]. http://www.ertico.com/about-ertico-its-glossary-glossary-01/.

[44] 徐飞跃,郭丽丽. 高等学校英语应用能力考试B级教程精编[M].上海:上海交通大学出版社,2012.

[45] 房思金,裘广宇. 高等学校英语应用能力考试教程[M].上海:上海交通大学出版社,2011.

[46] 裴玉龙,交通工程专业英语[M].北京:人民交通出版社,2002.

[47] 邬万江,马丽丽,交通工程专业英语[M].北京:机械工业出版社,2012.